AUSTRALIAN SHEPHERD BIBLE AND THE AUSTRALIAN SHEPHERD

Your Perfect Australian Shepherd Guide

COVERS AUSTRALIAN SHEPHERDS, AUSTRALIAN SHEPHERD PUPPIES, AUSTRALIAN SHEPHERD TRAINING, MINI AUSTRALIAN SHEPHERDS, AUSTRALIAN SHEPHERD BREEDERS, SIZE, HEALTH, MORE!

By Mark Manfield

© DYM Worldwide Publishers

DYM Worldwide Publishers

ISBN: 978-1-911355-55-7

for, the websites being temporarily or being removed from the Internet. The accuracy and completeness of the information provided herein and opinions stated herein are not guaranteed or warranted to produce any particular results, and the advice or strategies, contained herein may not be suitable for every individual. The author, publisher, distributors, and/or affiliates shall not be liable for any loss incurred as a consequence of the use and application, directly or indirectly of any information presented in this work. This publication is designed to provide information in regards to the subject matter covered. The information included in this book has been compiled to give an overview of the topics covered. The information contained in this book has been compiled to provide an overview of the subject. It is not intended as medical advice and should not be construed as such. For a firm diagnosis of any medical conditions you should consult a doctor or veterinarian (as related to animal health). The writer, publisher, distributors, and/or affiliates of this work are not responsible for any damages or negative consequences following any of the treatments or methods highlighted in this book. Website links are for informational purposes only and should not be seen as a personal endorsement; the same applies to any products or services mentioned in this work. The reader should also be aware that although the web links included were correct at the time of writing they may become out of date in the future. Any pricing or currency exchange rate information was accurate at the time of writing but may become out of date in the future. The Author, Publisher, distributors, and/or affiliates assume no responsibility for pricing and currency exchange rates mentioned within this work.

Table of Contents

Introduction

As the saying goes, a dog is man's best friend; but ask any dog lover, and he or she will say that dogs are more than that. Dogs can teach humans a thing or two about unconditional love, loyalty and positivity. They have the unique ability to lift our spirits without saying a word, and have the patience to be there for us when things are most difficult.

Having a dog is more than about ownership – it is about creating a relationship that will last for years and years to come. It is about love, nurturing and responsibility. It is about realizing that having a dog as a companion means that he or she becomes more than just a friend to you – he or she becomes part of your family.

The Australian Shepherd is one of the most loyal,
most energetic and smartest dog breeds out there.

If you've ever considered taking in a dog as part of your family,
you may have come across one of the smartest, most loyal, most
energetic and most adventurous breeds out there – the Australian
Shepherd or Aussie, for short.

Bred originally to herd livestock, the Australian Shepherd is
the happiest when he has a lot of work to do. An Australian
Shepherd rounding up a flock of sheep is certainly a marvelous
sight to behold. The dog moves with the surety of a professional
athlete, directing the flock with barks, nips and a penetrating gaze
that send the message to sheep that the Australian Shepherd is
the boss.

Loyal to his family but aloof towards strangers, Australian Shepherds thrive in homes that put his smarts and energy to good use. Of course, this does not mean that you have to own a flock of sheep if you want to welcome an Australian Shepherd into your family. What this does mean is that owning an Australian Shepherd means that you must keep him busy. The antithesis of a cat, this high-energy, spirited and hardworking dog would hate being stuck on the couch, sleeping and waking up just to eat before sleeping again.

Bred to herd, the Australian Shepherd
thrives when he or she has a job to do.

This breed has certainly a lot of energy to burn – so much so that a simple walk around the block might not cut it. The Australian Shepherd needs at least a small yard to run around and go crazy in. Without the space and without activities to do, this breed can become bored, loud and even destructive. Charmingly, this dog might create a job for himself if you have none lined up for him. He may take on jobs such as herding the kids, chasing other animals or even destroying the house if he feels like it. On the upside, the Australian Shepherd can be trained with some perseverance and patience, and can even be taught to do chores around the house such as picking up trash from the floor and putting it in the bin (you will still have to do the laundry yourself though).

While an energetic and lively dog certainly sounds like a positive, remember that you must have the time and energy to train and exercise the Australian Shepherd every day should you opt for this breed. If you would rather veg out in front of the television and sleep in all day during weekends, the Australian Shepherd will not be a good match for you.

However, while couch potatoes certainly won't find their spirit animal in the Australian Shepherd, those who are considering competitive dog shows may discover that this breed is the one for them. The Australian Shepherd is a stunner – with mid-length fur and eye color which range from dark brown yellow green, blue and even amber. Naturally athletic and agile, the Australian Shepherd is an awesome contender when it comes to obedience, flyball, herding and agility competitions. The breed has also proven to thrive in canine careers such as policing, search and rescue work, and guiding.

The Australian Shepherd is the perfect match for those with love adventure and physical activity.

Owning an Australian Shepherd can be both rewarding and challenging even for the most adventurous and active of people. What this book aims to do is to fully equip you with the necessary information so that you know what is entailed when it comes to owning a dog, much more owning an Australian Shepherd.

Aside from informing you where the Australian Shepherd originated and how a typical dog of this breed looks, succeeding chapters will educate you on: how to get ready for this new member of your family, how to deal with this breed's temperament, how to train your Australian Shepherd, how to properly nurture him, and so much more.

Read on and get to know more about the intelligent and spirited Australian Shepherd.

CHAPTER 1
Australian Shepherd History

With the Australian Shepherd's natural agility, energy and penchant for hard work, this dog is a desirable breed for adventurers and highly active individuals and families. Aside from its spirited nature, the Australian Shepherd's striking physicality and features also make this breed an attractive option for those seeking to welcome a dog into their family.

The history and origin of the Australian Shepherd
is not quite as clear as other breeds.

But while the reasons people opt for this breed is certainly apparent, the history of the Australian Shepherd isn't quite as direct and clear. As a matter of fact, the Australian Shepherd shouldn't even be referred to as an "Australian" or "Aussie".

In this chapter, not only will you learn why the Australian Shepherd shouldn't even be referred to as an "Australian", you will discover other breeds similar to the Australian – namely the Shetland Sheepdog and the Border Collie. Chapter 1 will help you get a bit more acquainted with the Australian Shepherd as well as learn their similarities and differences with the Shetland Sheepdog and Border Collie so you can make a better determination of whether the Aussie is the right breed for you and your family.

Australian Shepherd History

As mentioned, the origin and history of the Australian Shepherd are not quite as clear as other breeds. As a matter of fact, the breed was not recognized until the creation of the Australian Shepherd Club of America in 1957. The description of the breed and the basic features of the Australian Shepherd were not written until 1977. Moreover, the Australian Shepherd was not officially recognized as a breed by the American Kennel Club (SKC) until January 1, 1993.

The "Australian" in Australian Shepherd is a misnomer.
The breed is actually an American creation.

If the milestones mentioned above occurred only after the 1950s, what was occurring with the Australian Shepherd before then? You would be surprised to know that although the breed was only recognized with the creation of the Australian Shepherd Club of America in 1957, the Aussie had more likely been around even during the land rushes of the late 1800s.

The history and origin of the Aussie more likely began when European, Latin American and Australian settlers immigrated to North America, bringing along with them their herding dogs flocks of sheep. While shepherds from Australia did bring their sheep and herding dogs to North America, it is generally believed that Australian Shepherds more likely descended from herding dogs from Germany or the Basque Region of the Pyrenees Mountains.

While the wire-haired herding dogs from Germany and the Basque Region of the Pyrenees Mountains appeared to be smaller and leaner than Australian Shepherds, it is believed that these dogs were bred with other herding dogs to produce what is known today as the Aussie.

Although the history of the Australian Shepherd is mere speculation, once the dog breed did arrive in North America, they became prized for their sheep herding skills. They were initially bred more for function than form as they were primarily utilized as working farm dogs. There was no absolute standard for how the Australian Shepherd looked as their features were highly dependent on the terrain and weather conditions they were in. Instead, they were bred by American stockmen with practicality in mind. They were bred for their herding and guarding capabilities, exceptional intelligence, energy and alertness.

Fundamentally then, the Australian Shepherd is not Australian. It is actually an American breed bred by American stockmen. In fact, the breed is not recognized in Australia as a native breed.

Dogs Like Australian Shepherds: Comparing the Australian Shepherd and Shetland Sheepdogs – What are the Similarities and Differences?

The Australian Shepherd is a dog breed that is known to be intelligent, independent, loyal, alert and affectionate. The breed is known for its many talents such as retrieval, search and rescue, obedience, agility, guarding, herding and police work.

A typical Australian Shepherd weighs around 14-29 kilograms or 30-65 pounds and has a length that ranges from 43-66 centimeters or 17-26 inches. Having colors which range from black, liver, merle tan and white, it is common for this breed to have white trim or pigment on its body. However, if the dog has white on or around the ears, this is an indication that the dog has an increased risk of white-related deafness. Excessive white on the face and ears can also pose a greater risk of sunburn and skin cancer.

The lifespan of Aussies range from 13-15 years, and females typically have 3-10 puppies per litter. When it comes to health issues, the most common ones faced by Australian Shepherds are eye problems such as cataracts, red eye, epiphora and conjunctivitis, and dermatological and respiratory issues. Some Aussies are also susceptible to hip dysplasia as well as a genetic mutation of the MDR1 gene which puts them at a risk of suffering from toxicity from anti-parasitic drugs.

On the other hand, the Shetland Sheepdog or Sheltie is known to be playful, responsive, social, loving, gentle, affectionate and lively. Also deemed to be a breed of many talents, the Shetland

Sheepdog thrives when participating in activities such as obedience, agility, herding and guarding, and tracking.

The breed comes in a multitude of colors – tan and black, blue, brindle, merle, brown, tricolor, white and sable. Typically weighing around 5-11 kilograms or 11-24 pounds with a length of around 33-41 centimeters or 13-16 inches, Shetland Sheepdogs have a double coat, meaning their coat is made up of two layers of fur – the top of which contain long guard hairs and the bottom of which is made up of a thick, soft undercoat. The hair at the top layer repels water while the undercoat protects and provides relief to the dog when temperatures are both high and low.

The lifespan of Shetland Sheepdogs range from 12-13 years, and females typically have 4-6 puppies per litter. When it comes to health issues, Shelties are generally athletic and healthy; however, they can be susceptible to eye diseases, hypothyroidism, skin allergies, hip dysplasia and epilepsy. They are also four times more at risk of developing cancer of the bladder or transitional cell carcinoma.

While the Australian Shepherd and Shetland Sheepdog do have their similarities and differences when it comes to physical appearance, temperament and abilities, here are some of the things to consider when deciding on which dog breed is right for you and your family:

If you are an amateur dog owner, because Australian Sheepdogs tend to have more needs (especially when it comes to exercise and energy), Shetland Sheepdogs are better suited for first-time dog owners.

When it comes to the breeds' suitability for kids, both breeds are great with children, and have proven to be good and loyal family pets.

When it comes to maintenance, because its fur is mid-length, the Australian Shepherd is easier to maintain than the longer-haired Shetland Sheepdog. The Shetland Sheepdog tends to have more demanding, more time-consuming and more expensive grooming needs.

As for shedding, the longer-haired Shetland Sheepdog tends to shed more. This may be an issue especially for owners who are deterred from opting for pets due to shedding.

On the other hand, when it comes to training, Shetland Sheepdogs are easier to train since they tend to obey and listen more willingly. While the Australian Sheepdog is also trainable, they do tend to require more patience and perseverance due to their wanting to use their own smarts. Those who own Australian Shepherds may need to seek the help of obedience schools to train their dogs.

When it comes to their ability to protect and be watchdogs, both breeds have proven to make great watchdogs as they are extremely loyal to their families and have the instinct to bark and alert their owners when strangers arrive.

As for adaptability, Shetland Sheepdogs are more adaptable to their environment compared to Australian Shepherds.

When it comes to their need for exercise and activities, the energetic Australian Shepherd requires more exercise, thus making them the ideal dogs for adventurous people with active lifestyles.

Dogs Like Australian Shepherds: Comparing the Australian Shepherd and Border Collies – What are the Similarities and Differences?

As mentioned above, the Australian Shepherd is a breed known to be alert, energetic, independent, loyal, responsive and affectionate. For the Australian Shepherd to be healthy, this dog needs regular exercise. A dog that comes in black, liver, merle tan and white, the Australian Shepherd thrives when it participates in activities that have to do with search and rescue, retrieval, obedience, guarding and herding, narcotics detection and agility.

In general, an Australian Shepherd weighs around 14-29 kilograms or 30-65 pounds and has a length that ranges from 43-66 centimeters or 17-26 inches. The most common colors of Australian Shepherds are merle, black and red. It is common for this breed to have white trim or pigment on its body. However, as previously mentioned, take note if the dog has white on or around the ears. This is an indication that the dog has an increased risk of white-related deafness. Excessive white on the face and ears can also pose a greater risk of sunburn and skin cancer.

The lifespan of Aussies range from 13-15 years, and females typically have 3-10 puppies per litter. The most common health issues faced by Australian Shepherds, on the other hand, are eye problems such as cataracts, red eye, epiphora and conjunctivitis, and dermatological and respiratory issues. Some dogs of this breed are also susceptible to hip dysplasia and a genetic mutation of the MDR1 gene which puts them at a risk of suffering from toxicity from anti-parasitic drugs.

On the other hand, the Border Collie is known for being loyal, responsive, protective, alert and intelligent. Like the Australian Shepherd, the Border Collie requires regular exercise to remain healthy. It also thrives in activities that involve search and rescue, retrieval, obedience, guarding and herding, narcotics detection and agility.

Like the Shetland Sheepdog, the Border Collie also has a double coat which can be smooth or rough and can also be curled. The Border Collie comes in a multitude of colors such as liver, lilac merle, chocolate, blue, black, white, red, brindle, sable, and sable merle. Also, a typical Border Collie will have a length of anywhere from 46-56 centimeters or 18-22 inches and weigh around 12-20 kilograms or 26-44 pounds.

Typically, Border Collie females will have a maximum of 10 puppies per litter. And when it comes to its lifespan, Border Collies can live from 10-14 years. The common afflictions of this dog breed include epilepsy, hip dysplasia and Collie eye anomaly (CEA) which is an inherited eye disease that affects the retina, choroid and sclera.

While the Australian Shepherd and Border Collie do have their similarities and differences when it comes to physical appearance, temperament and abilities, here are some of the things to consider when deciding on which dog breed is right for you and your family:

If you are an amateur dog owner, like the Shetland Sheepdog, the Border Collie is a better option for first-time dog owners when compared to the Australian Shepherd. This is because Australian Sheepdogs tend to have more needs (especially when it comes to exercise and energy).

When it comes to the breeds' suitability for kids, both breeds are great with children, and have proven to be good and loyal family pets.

When it comes to maintenance, the Australian Shepherd and Border Collie both require moderate maintenance. These two breeds may require somewhat demanding grooming regimens, depending on whether they are made to compete in dog shows or not.

As for shedding, both dogs tend to shed moderately. To prevent further shedding, dog owners of both breeds are encouraged to brush their fur regularly.

On the other hand, when it comes to training, Border Collies are easier to train since they tend to obey and listen more willingly. While the Australian Sheepdog is also trainable, they do tend to require more patience and perseverance due to their wanting to use their own smarts. Those who own Australian Shepherds may need to seek the help of obedience schools to train their dogs.

When it comes to their ability to protect and be watchdogs, both breeds have proven to make great watchdogs as they are extremely loyal to their families and have the instinct to bark and alert their owners when strangers arrive.

As for adaptability, Australian Shepherds and Border Collies have the same level of adaptability.

When it comes to their need for exercise and activities, both breeds require strenuous daily exercise to keep healthy.

CHAPTER 2

The Characteristics of the Australian Shepherd

I f you believe that the Australian Shepherd is a good fit for you and your family over the other breeds mentioned above, this chapter will help you find out how to spot a purebred Australian Shepherd. For first-time and aspiring dog owners, the physical characteristics and colors of the Australian Shepherd can help you make a determination of whether a dog is purebred or not. Also, this chapter seeks to answer whether a miniature or teacup Australian Shepherd truly exists.

This chapter will also outline for you the temperament of the Australian Shepherd. As a preview, it has repeatedly been mentioned previously that this dog breed is smart, loyal and extremely energetic! If you want to welcome an Australian Shepherd into your home, be prepared for a whole lot of activity and energy!

How to Spot a Purebred Australian Shepherd

Flecks on the body are some of the easiest ways to determine if a dog is a purebred Australian Shepherd.

While Australian Shepherds come in various colors, the easiest way to determine whether the dog is a purebred Australian Shepherd is to check for ticking. A common pattern in Australian Shepherds, ticking is the presence of spots or flecks on colors in white areas of the dog's body. In as much as white markings are like white paint over a dog to obscure its true color, tick marks can be seen as finger smudges in the white paint to reveal the color underneath.

Considered as an inherited simple dominant gene, the size, number and roundness of ticks are determined by modifiers. While ticking is obvious when white areas are apparent in dogs, when the animal is black or tan and lacks white areas, ticks may still be present but are not seen. In Australian Shepherds, ticking may be present even in solid-colored and merle dogs.

Tick marks in Australian Shepherds can look like small flecks or freckles, or can be big and round and the size of nickels.

While ticking is an indication of a purebred Australian Shepherd, the following are steps you can take to truly make a determination if the dog you are opting for is a purebred:

Make sure you do your research.

Before you adopt or purchase an Australian Shepherd, make sure you know what apparent physical features to watch out for. Do your research and make a determination of what makes Australian Shepherds different from other breeds. Know how they look and what sets them apart from others so that you can deter scammers from tricking you.

Doing the necessary research will also help you come up with vital questions you can ask breeders about Australian Shepherds. You can ask breeders questions such as the proper diet you can feed your dog, or how much exercise Australian Shepherds need per day.

Know how to spot an Australian Shepherd.

Do you know how an Australian Shepherd looks like? Can you spot an Australian Shepherd puppy from a litter of other herding dogs? Knowing how to spot an Australian Shepherd will prevent you from being scammed into adopting non-purebreds or another breed. Know what the defining features of an Australian Shepherd are.

Remember that Australian Shepherds are athletic dogs of medium size and are slightly longer than they are tall. These dogs come in a variety of colors – namely, black, liver, merle tan and white. Also, purebred Australian Shepherds will have white markings or tickings on the face, chest, and or legs.

Only do business with a reputable breeder.

Do your research and only do business with reputable breeders. Trustworthy breeders will not only have the necessary paperwork and photos about their dogs, but they will also be able to be upfront with you about the health concerns of their animals as well as the pros and cons of owning an Australian Shepherd. Reputable breeders will have no reason to fool you, while scammers will try to only give you the positives of the animals they are selling.

Knowing how to determine whether an Australian Shepherd breeder is reputable will be further discussed in a separate chapter.

If a deal is too good to be true, it is more likely too good to be true.

Be careful of breeders selling Australian Shepherds at a low price. Purebred Australian Shepherds can be rather pricey. If a breeder is selling his or her dogs at a very low price, this could be a sign that his or her animals are unhealthy or are not purebred.

Australian Shepherd Types - Australian Shepherd Colors: Black Australian Shepherd and Red Australian Shepherd, Tan and White

The breed standards for Australian Shepherds state that the breed can come in a combination of two basic colors (black and liver), one pattern (merle) and two trim colors (white and tan).

Australian Shepherds can come in two trim colors, one pattern or two basic colors such as black and liver.

Black and Liver (Red)

Black is the dominant trait to liver. This means that a liver-colored dog will only produce liver-colored puppies when bred with another liver-colored dog. However, black Australian Shepherds can produce puppies that are either black or liver depending on whether they carry the liver gene referred to as "red factored." If a black Australian Shepherd does not have the liver gene, it will never produce liver-colored puppies.

Tan

Tan trims or points are caused by one of several versions of the gene Agouti. Two of these versions contribute to the normal coat color of Australian Shepherds, one of which gives the dog breed a tan coloring while the other does not. However, when an Australian Shepherd has the dominant gene referred to as K, the dog will not have a tan trim. This then means that the tan trim or point can either be dominant or recessive, depending on the version of agouti or K the dog has in his genetic makeup.

White

Considered as the most genetically complex of the normal Australian Shepherd color, the general rule is that the dog breed tends to have less white than more. Having less white markings tend to be more dominant than having more. This means that two dogs with little white markings can produce puppies with a lot of white, but a pair that has the maximum white trim will not produce puppies with almost none.

The Merle Australian Shepherd: The Blue Merle Australian Shepherd and Red Merle Australian Shepherd, and Double Merles

Before we go talk about the Blue Merle Australian Shepherd and Red Merle Australian Shepherd, let's first answer what a merle is.

The merle is a color pattern, not a color. Merle Australian Shepherds can come in different colors. This pattern makes dogs of the same breed look different from each other because puppies from the same litter could have different patterns and colors. While some may have blue patches throughout their bodies, other Australian Shepherds could have patterns of red and tan. The merle gene creates patches of color in a solid-colored coat and can affect skin pigment as well. Because health issues can arise if two merle dogs are bred together, it is highly recommended that a merle Australian Shepherd only be bred with a solid colored Australian Shepherd only.

The Blue Merle Australian Shepherd and Red Merle Australian Shepherd

While the Blue Merle Australian Shepherd is a black dog with its black being broken up into irregularly shaped patches of gray, a Red Merle Australian Shepherd is a liver/red dog with irregularly shaped patches of tan. These merle patterns can vary from very light to very dark, and some dogs may be heavily merled while others may only have a few patches. Merle patterns can also come in a variety of other colors aside from just mere gradations. These include dilute red or blue, fawn, sable and yellow.

Another version of the merle gene produces Australian Shepherds that are "phantom (or cryptic) merles". These dogs appear to be one solid color at first glance; however, they are genetically merle dogs and produce puppies that have the merle pattern.

Double Merles

Australian Shepherds are referred to as "double merles" when they have two copies of the merle version of a gene called Silv.

Dogs that are double merles usually have eyes that develop abnormally or will be blind.

Aside from blindness or abnormal eyes and eyesight, double merles can also be deaf because of the lack of pigment in the inner ear. As mentioned previously, white markings or tickings on or around the ear can connote some form of deafness, and the same mechanism can lead to deafness in double merles although it is with a different genetic base.

Some people refer to these dogs as "lethal whites", thinking that double merles have genetic issues that cause the animals to pass away before they reach an age which they can reproduce. However, this is not the case for the Australian Shepherd double merles. But while this is not the case for double merles, these dogs do have serious health issues and disabilities and should not be bred. Double merles will be discussed further later on in this e-book.

Size of Australian Shepherd and Physical Characteristics: What Does an Australian Shepherd Look Like, Australian Shepherd Average Weight and Other Features

Considered to be an athletic breed, the Australian Shepherd comes in striking coat colors and eye colors.

The Australian Shepherd is considered to be a medium-sized breed with a solid, athletic build. When it comes to weight, these dogs can weigh anywhere from 14-29 kilograms or 30-65 pounds. According to the Australian Shepherd Club of America (ASCA), the standard for the Australian Shepherd is that the breed stands between 18 and 23 inches (46 and 58 cm) at the withers, with females measuring 18 to 21 inches (46 to 53 cm) and males measuring 20 to 23 inches (51 to 58 cm). The ASCA, however, states that the quality of the dog should not be sacrificed for the size.

While the Australian Shepherd can come in solid colors, they are best known for their striking merle coat which gives the dog breed a marbled appearance. Aside from their striking coat colors and patterns, the range of eye colors this dog breed can come in is equally beautiful. Australian Shepherds can have brown, amber, hazel, blue or green eyes, and may even have two eyes of different colors (one green and one blue, for example) or even "split" eyes with half of one eye being one color and the other half being another color.

When it comes to their tails, some Australian Shepherds have full long tails, others have naturally bobbed tails and others have natural partial bobs (tail is shorter and stubby).

Understanding the Australian Shepherd Temperament

As previously mentioned, the Australian Shepherd is a highly intelligent, spirited, athletic, hardworking and energetic breed. Requiring a great deal of attention and daily exercise, the Australian Shepherd truly thrives when he is put to work, when he is learning and practicing tricks, competing and/or engaging in mental and physical activities. When this dog breed is not able to involve in the activities he thrives in, he may become destructive or may "invent" his own activities or roles which may be undesirable to his owner/s. For example, when an Australian Shepherd is not given the exercise or activities it requires he may take it upon himself to chase cars or other animals, or even herd the children in the family.

With a reputation for being hard working and versatile, the Australian Shepherd is an ideal dog when it comes to working with livestock such as rabbits, ducks, geese and sheep. They thrive in rural, farm-like environments with a lot of wide, open spaces. However, the Australian Shepherd can still thrive in an urban environment for as long as the dog has access to a spacious yard. Remember, however, that it is not enough to simply give them space. This dog breed needs training and activities to keep it focused and happy.

Also, this dog breed needs plenty of human companionship. This need for constant interaction has led to them being referred to as "Velcro dogs" as they have a tendency to develop intense and strong bonds with select people.

Extremely loyal, devoted, kind and loving to his owner/s, the Australian Shepherd can be a cautious watchdog. Because this dog breed was bred to serve on ranches, the Australian Shepherd has developed a protectiveness of property, leading its inclination to bark warnings when strangers are approaching. The fortunate thing, however, is that the dog breed is not inclined to bark excessively.

Miniature Australian Shepherd and Teacup Australian Shepherd – Do They Exist?

The simple answer to whether Miniature Australian Shepherd and Teacup Australian Shepherd exist is yes; however, whether they (the Teacup Australian Shepherd in particular) should exist in the first place is controversial.

The Miniature Australian Shepherd and Teacup Australian Shepherd had their beginnings in the late 1960s when a breeder opted to start a program which sought to create smaller versions of the standard Australian Shepherd. Australian Shepherds do not always come in the same size, so the breeder chose the smallest members to breed. From the smaller breeds, small dogs were produced which were in turn, bred, and consequently produced smaller dogs. This resulted in the creation of the Miniature Australian Shepherd which usually weighs anywhere between 15 and 35 pounds with a length of around 13 to 18 inches. The Miniature Australian Shepherd was similar in almost all aspects to the standard Australian Shepherd. The main difference between the two was just the size.

More than the Miniature Australian Shepherd, the source of contention amongst breeders is the Teacup Australian Shepherd which is an exceptionally small dog. Weighing only 4 to 8 pounds with a length of only 8 to 10 inches, the Teacup Australian Shepherd is being deemed by some breeders and pet owners as a totally separate breed from the standard Australian Shepherd. Aside from the size, the Teacup Australian Shepherd has a very different temperament to the standard Australian Shepherd. The teacup version of the dog breed is not deemed as a working dog, more inclined to fear-biting, more high-strung and yappy. Aside from a different temperament, the reason why others do not approve of breeding the teacup variety is that they have particular health issues not found in standard Australian Shepherds. Making them a lot more fragile, these health issues are brought about by inbreeding and breeding smaller dogs which are more likely to be less healthy than normal sized ones.

CHAPTER 3

Committing to Owning the Australian Shepherd Dog Breed

Welcoming an Australian Shepherd into your family sounds good, but are you truly ready to care for and love this dog for years to come? Remember, that a dog is not a toy. A dog is a living, loving creature who seeks a good and caring home and family. Owning a dog is a long-term commitment that should be entered into willingly and with full understanding.

Before opting to adopt or buy an Australian Shepherd, this chapter features some of the most common questions you might want to ask yourself when it comes to committing to owning this breed.

Is the Australian Shepherd a Good Fit for You or Your Family?

Before committing to owning an Australian Shepherd, know that it is a dominant dog that needs daily exercise.

While the Australian Shepherd is certainly a great dog breed, ask yourself whether or not it is a good fit for you or your family.

Here are some of the considerations you may want to keep in mind:

The Australian Shepherd's temperament.

Dominant and inclined to be controlling because they were bred to be so, the Australian Shepherd will attempt to control you. Decipher your personality and whether you can manage to continue on being the alpha dog of your household. If you feel that you may not be able to take leadership of your household

with the Australian Shepherd's personality, either opt fc
breed or be prepared to be bossed around by your prosp

Australian Shepherds need ongoing training and daily exercise.

While puppy training is sufficient for other breeds, training for Australian Shepherds will be ongoing until adulthood. They also need daily exercise or else they might get destructive. This will require you to commit your time and energy to ensuring that your dog gets the training he or she requires.

Australian Shepherds can become clingy.

This dog breed can get very attached to select people and need constant attention. These dogs can literally walk so close to you that you might end up entangling yourself on them, leading you both to get toppled over.

If you are too busy for this breed, remember that they can get into mischief when left to their own devices. They will think of ways to fill the lonely hours while you are away.

The Australian Shepherd is not a starter dog.

Australian Shepherds can be a handful and they can be extremely challenging. If you have never owned a dog before, an Australian Shepherd may prove to be too difficult to handle. While Australian Shepherds are good with children, they are not toys. They need strong leadership because they have a mind of their own.

Is Your Home Suitable for an Australian Shepherd?

The main thing to take into consideration regarding Australian Shepherds and the dog breed's suitability to your home is space. Not only do Australian Shepherds love to exercise, but they also need it. Your home must have enough space to allow your dog to have enough regular rigorous exercise. They do not thrive in small spaces or apartments with no yard. Make sure you have access to a park or a spacious yard if you opt to own an Australian Shepherd. Without the necessary exercise, your dog's demeanor will change. Their usual pleasant character will shift and progress from boredom, restlessness, frustration and short-temperedness.

Are Australian Shepherds Aggressive Towards People?

Extremely protective of their territory and family, Australian Shepherds are wary of strangers. This then means that this breed needs to be properly socialized from when these dogs are puppies. If you do not socialize your dog properly, you may end up with a dog that is aggressive towards other people. They can become fearful of other people who are not members of their family, and dogs that are fearful usually express this fear through aggression.

Are Australian Shepherds Aggressive Towards Other Dogs?

Australian Shepherds can also be aggressive towards other dogs if they are not properly socialized from when they are puppies. You should be cautious of aggression towards other dogs of the same sex as your Australian Shepherd.

When it comes to aggression towards other dogs, here are some distinctive characteristics your Australian Shepherd can demonstrate:

1. Bullying other dogs through poking, nudging and barking.
2. Assuming an aggressive stance when meeting new dogs. This involves raising his head high and staring, with ears pricked and tail tensed and raised high.

Are Australian Shepherds Aggressive Towards Other Animals?

Bred to be a working dog that is hardwired to herd cattle and other livestock, Australian Shepherds are inclined to being aggressive towards other animals. After all, their primary method of herding livestock is to chase and nip, as well as to protect their herd from strange animals and predators.

The best ways to prevent aggression is through socialization from a young age, proper training, ensuring that your dog gets the rigorous exercise he needs, possibly neutering male Australian Shepherds, and even reducing aggression-causing excess protein from their diet.

How Big Do Australian Shepherds Get?

*The standard Australian Shepherd can weigh
anywhere from 14-29 kilograms or 30-65 pounds.*

As mentioned, the standard Australian Shepherd can weigh anywhere from 14-29 kilograms or 30-65 pounds. According to the Australian Shepherd Club of America (ASCA), the standard for the Australian Shepherd is that the breed stands between 18 and 23 inches (46 and 58 cm) at the withers, with females measuring 18 to 21 inches (46 to 53 cm) and males measuring 20 to 23 inches (51 to 58 cm).

On the other hand, the Miniature Australian Shepherd usually weighs anywhere between 15 and 35 pounds with a length of around 13 to 18 inches; while the Teacup Australian Shepherd weighs only 4 to 8 pounds with a length of only 8 to 10 inches.

Does the Australian Shepherd Dog Breed Have Any Serious Genetic Health Issues?

Yes, the Australian Shepherd can have serious genetic health issues that could potentially have an enormous impact on the breed as puppies or even on adult dogs later in life.

Some of the serious genetic hereditary health conditions include: cataracts, cancer, allergies, epilepsy, hip dysplasia, autoimmune diseases, iris coloboma (gap or hole in one of the structures of the eye), Colie Eye Anomaly (or CEA which is an abnormality of the choroid or sclera), undescended testicles, distichiasis (eyelashes grow inward), and others.

Because of these potential serious genetic health issues, it is important to do business with a reputable breeder so that you find the most suitable pet for you, and so that you are as informed as you can be when making the life-changing decision of owning an Australian Shepherd.

What Are the Pros and Cons of Having an Australian Shepherd?

Just like any other dog breed, there are pros and cons to owning an Australian Shepherd. Here are some of them:

Pros

1. Australian Shepherds have a penchant for play. They never seem to lose this puppy-like quality. This is the reason why they are great dogs to have if you have children. They make great pets for as long as they are socialized properly from when they are puppies.

2. Australian Shepherds are highly intelligent and thrive when trained.

3. They are devoted and loyal to their family. They make great watchdogs since they are naturally inclined to protecting their herd or pack, as well as turf.

4. This dog breed is striking. Australian Shepherds come in a variety of colors, some which have a distinctive marbling or merle to their coats.

Cons

1. If you lead a busy lifestyle, an Australian Shepherd may prove to be just too much work for you. This breed needs daily exercise and constant training and attention. If you have the willingness, time and energy to give your dog what he requires, then this will be a pro for you.

2. Because Australian Shepherds are highly intelligent and dominant, they have a tendency of wanting and trying to be the boss of the household. However, if you can show leadership, your dog will show you respect and see you as the alpha dog of the pack. This is done through proper training from the get-go.

3. Australian Shepherds need a lot of space to expend their energy. If you do not have much space, this breed is not the one for you.

4. While Australian Shepherds may be hardy and athletic animals, a gene found in merle dogs can cause deafness or blindness. Dogs with bobtails can also develop serious spinal defects.

Am I Truly Ready to Own an Australian Shepherd?

You may truly want a pet, but are you truly ready to own one? Wanting and being ready are two very different things. This is a very important question to ask yourself before you go out and purchase an Australian Shepherd, adopt or rescue one.

Here are some of the things that you need to consider or ask yourself to make sure that you are ready and willing to commit to owning a dog:

1. Your dog will live for around 13-15 years, do you foresee any major changes happening to you during your pet's lifetime? Changes could be anything from getting a new job, moving overseas, getting married and having children. Should these changes occur, do you think you will still be willing to spend the necessary time, money and energy to take care of your beloved Australian Shepherd?

2. If you have children, married or live with a partner, or have other pets, what will you do if they are allergic to your dog or they simply cannot get along with your Australian Shepherd?

3. If you are thinking of purchasing or adopting a dog for your children so they can have a pet, are you willing and able to take on the responsibility of nurturing and caring for the pet if your children lose interest, move away or grow up?

4. Are you a new pet owner, and have you asked other more experienced pet owners on how to take care of dogs? Did you do the necessary research regarding dogs, and more specifically, Australian Shepherds?

5. Have you owned a pet in the past that died due to a preventable illness or disease such as heartworm or being hit by a car? If you have answered yes, what will you do differently if you acquire a new pet?

CHAPTER 4
Australian Shepherd Breeders

When you have decided to welcome an Australian Shepherd into your home and family, one of the biggest decisions you will make is whether to buy a puppy from a breeder or adopt a dog from a shelter or recue group.

Do the necessary research before doing business with a breeder or adopting from a shelter.

🐕 51

Before you make a decision regarding where you want to get your prospective pet from, make sure to do the necessary research. Read on. This chapter delves into some considerations and tips you need to make the best decision possible when it comes to purchasing an Australian Shepherd, deciphering whether a breeder is legitimate or not, and whether you should opt for a shelter or rescue dog.

Australian Shepherd for Sale: Buying an Australian Shepherd from a Breeder vs. Other Options – Which Should You Choose?

There are different ways of acquiring an Australian Shepherd – the two main ways of which are buying from a breeder and adopting from a shelter or rescue group. Which of the two is the best for you?

Before delving into these two options, know to never buy from a puppy mill. Puppy mills are large dog breeding facilities that prioritize profit over the well-being and health of the dogs. Also, be wary of purchasing dogs from pet stores as many of the puppies they sell also come from puppy mills.

So, what is the best option when it comes to acquiring an Australian Shepherd (or any dog for that matter)? It will depend on your purpose as a dog owner, and on what it is you are looking for and are ready for.

Buying from a Breeder

If you are thinking about acquiring a puppy from a breeder, first make sure that you choose a reputable breeder. Determining what makes a breeder reputable will be discussed later.

Some of the benefits that go with purchasing a puppy from a breeder are:

- You will see your puppy's parents as well as the environment in which your prospective pet was raised.
- Reputable breeders will give you all the necessary information you need regarding the puppy you want to buy. This includes genetic health testing information to ensure that your prospective pet is not likely to carry any inherited genetic health issues.
- You know exactly what you are getting yourself into when it comes to the dog breed.
- Because breeders typically sell puppies, owning a puppy will give you the opportunity to raise your dog into the type of pet you want him to be through consistent socialization and training.

However, the following are the challenges that go with buying a puppy from a breeder:

- Puppies require a lot of work – after all, they are just babies and require a lot of cleaning up after, comforting, and others.
- You are responsible for making sure that your puppy is socialized and trained so that he grows up properly.
- Purebred dogs usually have more health problems.
- Purchasing a puppy can be extremely expensive and you will be responsible for the vetting of your pet.

Adopting a Dog from a Shelter or Rescue Group

There continues to be a stigma that rescue and shelter dogs are unpredictable and have behavioral issues. However, these are misconceptions. A good number of dogs that are given to shelters because of changes in family situations and not because of behavioral problems. Also, some of them may already have some training.

Some of the benefits that go with adopting a dog from a shelter or rescue group are:

- Not only are you able to free up more space in the rescue or shelter for another dog, but you are able to save the life of the dog you adopt.
- Most of these dogs have already had their vetting completed which includes spaying or neutering and microchipping.
- It's less expensive to adopt rather than to buy from a breeder. A good number of shelters only charge $150 adoption fee which includes the cost of temporary housing in the shelter, food, microchipping, sterilization, medical evaluation and necessary medication.
- There are no surprises when you adopt a dog from a rescue group because personnel can tell you about your prospective pet's personality.
- A lot of the adult dogs are already potty-trained.
- Mixed breeds tend to have less inherited genetic health issues.
- The love and gratitude you receive from your rescue or shelter dog are priceless.

However, the following are the challenges that go with adopting a dog from a shelter or rescue group:

- Although there are purebred dogs in shelters, there are some dogs whose breeds are unknowable.

- Rescue or shelter dogs are older and may already be set in their ways.

- These dogs may come with "baggage" which leads them to be fearful and anxious. Training or teaching them to trust you may prove to be challenging and may take a while.

- Some rescue dogs suffer from separation anxiety and may become destructive when left alone.

Breeding Australian Shepherds: How to Find and Recognize Good Australian Shepherd Breeders

A good breeder will want the best for his or her dogs.

If you are opting to buy an Australian Shepherd from a breeder, take the time to research breeders in your area. Not only are you protecting yourself and your family from heartache and disappointment, but you are also protecting the breed itself by making sure you only deal with breeders who really care about the Australian Shepherd and seek to eliminate shattering genetic problems in their dogs.

Remember that deciding based on price will more likely lead to trouble and devastation. Don't scrimp just to save a few dollars; this will only more likely lead to you spending more on veterinary bills and will only lead to heartbreak if you get attached to a pet that has a lot of health issues.

These are some of the things to look for in an Australian Shepherd breeder to make sure that he or she is reputable:

1. Loves his or her dogs and the breed, and makes dog breeding his or her life work.

A reputable Australian Shepherd breeder will not only love his or her dogs, but he or she will also be passionate about the breed. His or her dogs and puppies represent his or her life work, and he or she does everything he or she can to improve the overall dog breed.

He or she will encourage you to come to his or her facilities so that you can see the dogs for yourself and the environment in which they live. The facility is usually the breeder's home; but whether the facility is the breeder's home itself, it will always be clean and spacious and the breeder's dogs will always be properly trained and socialized. It will be obvious that the breeder interacts with the dogs daily and has a bond with them.

While profit is something that all people who go into business are concerned about, a reputable breeder will always put the best interest of the breed before making money. They will always opt for high quality over quantity.

2. Only breeds Australian Shepherds, or breeds Aussies plus one other breed.

Reputable breeders do this because they want to be extremely knowledgeable in the dog breed they want to get involved with. Puppy mills and bad breeders do not care about the breed because all they really want to do is earn as much profit as possible.

3. Asks you as many questions as you ask him or her, and makes sure you can provide his or her puppy with a good home.

A reputable breeder will only sell his or her puppies to people and families they meet in person. They do not ship them off to pet stores or other places wherein the fate of the puppy is not known.

He or she will also ask you questions about your experiences with dogs and about your home environment. Some even opt to visit your home so that they are sure that you can provide their puppies with a good home.

After the sale, breeders will keep lines of communication open with you just in case you have any questions when it comes to raising your Australian Shepherd.

4. Will provide a written contract and health guarantee.

A good breeder will provide papers to show you that your puppy is healthy, and will ask you to sign a contract that states that you can return the dog back to him or her at any point in the dog's life if you are unable to take care of the animal anymore.

5. Can show you pedigrees for both parents usually for at least three generations of healthy Australian Shepherds.

A reputable breeder can tell you the genetic issues found in Australian Shepherds and can provide proof that the parents and grandparents of your puppy have been evaluated with the intention of eliminating these health issues from the line's gene pool.

6. Can refer you to a good local vet, and can get you in touch with other families who have adopted his or her puppies.

These referrals and references will be extremely useful to you and will help build trust between you and the dog breeder. Not only will you discover the legitimacy of the breeder, but the breeder is also assured that you seek the betterment of your puppy.

7. Has a waiting list.

Breeders don't always have puppies available because they will give their dogs a break from parenthood. A reputable breeder will have a waiting list for future litters.

8. Is registered with organizations such as the American Kennel Club (AKC) or Australian Shepherd Club of America (ASCA).

These reliable organizations will not recommend bad breeders, and are extremely strict and cautious when it comes to standards and safety practices when it comes to the dog breed and breeding. You can trust whatever these organizations have to say.

The Telltale Signs of Bad Australian Shepherd Breeders

While the characteristics that make up good Australian Shepherd breeders were previously mentioned, there are also telltale signs when it comes to bad Australian Shepherd breeders. These include the following:

1. Concern for profit over the well-being of the dogs.

A bad breeder will be more concerned about the money he or she will be earning from the dogs rather than the well-being and health of the dogs. He or she will not provide a clean and spacious environment for his or her dogs, he or she will not care about where the dogs will go after the sale, and he or she does not interact or bond with the dogs due to lack of concern for them.

2. Will sell you any breed.

A bad breeder will offer and sell you any type of breed – from Australian Shepherds to French Bulldogs to Poodles to dogs that he or she does not even know the breed. His or her concern is quantity over quality and could care less about being knowledgeable about the dogs in his or her care. Being selective is not a priority as a bad breeder will want to have whatever breed his or her client is looking for.

3. Do not have policies when it comes to refunds or replacements.

Bad breeders do not want to see the dog they sell to you so they have no policies or guarantees when it comes to refunds or replacements. All they care about is making a sale.

4. Does not make you sign a contract.

Contracts protect both you and the breeder. Bad breeders do not want contracts because they don't really care about the animals they have. Should you be unable to care for the dog in the future due to changes in your circumstances, they do not want to have anything to do with the animal.

5. Does not want you to visit his or her facility.

Be extremely suspicious if the breeder does not want you to see the dogs and the animals they live in. These breeders may be running puppy mills or providing insufficient care to the dogs. The bad dog breeders may sell ill puppies or those who may have been treated cruelly.

6. Can't guarantee the health of the puppy.

Bad breeders cannot guarantee the health of their puppies because they do not want to spend their money to ensure that their animals are not ill or have any genetic health issues. They may even be guilty of breeding incompatible dogs who then produces litters with devastating genetic abnormalities. For example, in Australian Shepherds, bad and ignorant breeders may continue breeding two dogs with merle patterns for aesthetics' sake even though they produce puppies that could potentially be deaf or blind.

7. Has no papers for the puppy.

While good breeders can demonstrate and provide you papers when it comes to the pedigree of their puppies, bad breeders cannot. They have no actual papers to show you and simply try to reel you in by asking for a lower price for their puppies.

8. Cannot provide references and referrals.

They are not registered with any dog breed organization and are not able to provide you with references when it comes to local vets. Also, they will not be able to provide client referrals so you can ask regarding previously purchased puppies.

Australian Shepherd Adoption: Australian Shepherd Rescue Myths and Misconceptions

Previously, the benefits and challenges of adopting or rescuing Australian Shepherds were discussed. In this section, the topic of adoption and rescue will be further discussed by addressing common myths and misconceptions about shelter and rescue dogs in general. Here are some of these common myths and misconceptions:

1. Dogs from shelters and rescue groups are mutts.

While it is certainly true that some dogs in shelters and rescue groups are from questionable gene pools, this generalization is not always true. There are a good number of people who purchase dogs from reputable breeders and pet stores who later decide that they are unable to care for the animals. As a matter of fact, The Humane Society estimates that around 25% of dogs in shelters and rescue groups are purebred.

Also, if there is a specific breed that you want to adopt, there are breed-specific groups out there that rescue their chosen breeds from shelters. In the case of Australian Shepherds, you can get more information regarding Australian Shepherd adoption through groups such as the Aussie Rescue and Placement Helpline (ARPH).

2. Dogs are placed in shelters and given to rescue groups because there is something wrong with them.

While there are some dogs in shelters and rescue groups that have behavioral issues, most are simply there due to the changes in their owners' personal circumstances such as job loss, death, evictions, divorce, moving overseas and simply being incapable of caring for them.

3. Dogs in shelters are too old.

There are a lot of adult dogs in shelters; but believe it or not, there are also a lot of puppies. Dogs of all ages reside in shelters and are rescued by concerned groups and organizations.

But, do not discount senior dogs altogether. A lower-energy household might enjoy having an older dog rather than a puppy. Reasons for this will more likely be because older dogs require less constant attention and are unlikely to need toilet training. Plus, the old saying that older dogs cannot learn new tricks is untrue.

4. Dogs in shelters are dirty.

Shelters are not puppy mills. The people who work in these institutions care about the dogs in their care. Many have groomers who come in on a regular basis and help groom the dogs. Volunteers also give their time to make sure that dogs are brushed and trained, as well as treated for ticks and fleas.

CHAPTER 5

Choosing an Australian Shepherd for Your Family

You know you want an Australian Shepherd. You've talked with a breeder about purchasing a puppy from him or her, or you've decided on adopting a rescue dog. However, you still want to learn more about choosing the right Australian Shepherd for your family.

Ask yourself some vital questions before acquiring an Australian Shepherd.

Now that you're becoming more aware of the options available to you when it comes to acquiring your Australian Shepherd, this chapter provides you with some more questions you need to ask yourself to find the most suitable dog for you and your family.

Australian Shepherd Puppies versus Australian Shepherd Adult?

While puppies are certainly some of the cutest creatures around, expect that you will be spending a lot of time and energy on them during their first year of life. Like babies, they need constant attention, nurturing, teaching and molding.

Both adult dogs and puppies have their pros and cons.

An adult dog, on the other hand, does away with all that training and you skip the developmental stages which can prove to be tiring and exhausting. However, you might want to be part of those developmental stages. You may want to see your pet grow up and you may want to have your pet as part of your life for longer. Although adult dogs are still trainable, they may already be set in their ways.

Both puppies and adult dogs have their benefits and drawbacks. Before you opt for one over the other, you may want to ask yourself the following questions:

1. How much time and energy can you dedicate to your Australian Shepherd?

Puppies require constant supervision during their first year of life. You will need to constantly take them out every few hours so they can relieve themselves. You need to socialize and lay down the basics of obedience training properly. A puppy's developmental stages are the times wherein you need to make sure that he or she has a good solid foundation when it comes to good behavior.

Adult dogs, on the other hand, may have already been trained when they were puppies. You no longer need to worry about laying out a solid foundation for them. All you should do is be consistent and to follow through with this training.

If your schedule is flexible and you have and are willing to spend a lot of time and energy on your pet, a puppy may be for you. However, if you want a pet that is already housetrained, an adult dog may be more suitable for you and your family.

2. How important is it for you to be able to raise your dog and mold his or her personality?

Raising a puppy allows you to help in the formation of his or her personality and behavior. On the other hand, the personality of an adult dog has already been formed by his or her previous owner; therefore, how good he or she behaves is dependent of how he or she was treated previously. If you want to be able to mold your pet to fit your home and family from the get-go, go with a puppy; however, if this does not matter to you, go with an adult dog.

3. Is cost an issue?

Both puppies and adult dogs have costs that are associated with them. Puppies tend to cost more than adult dogs when you purchase them. Also, both have different veterinary costs that you need to be responsible for – although adult dogs that are not too old tend to be sturdier and more solid than puppies if they are not already ill or suffer from genetic health conditions.

Should You Choose a Male or Female?

You've decided on an Australian Shepherd, but have you decided on what sex you should get? In as much as human beings have to contend with the battle of the sexes, many swear that there is a distinction between male and female dogs. Male dogs are said to be more affectionate but hardheaded, while female dogs tend to be more protective of their families and owners and are therefore more aggressive. However, this belief is not a definite truth – after all, the behavior of dogs is deeply dependent on how they were socialized, trained and raised as puppies.

While the behavior of dogs is dependent on their training, the sex of the animal does dictate its ability to learn from training. Factually, the female dog will be smaller in size than males and tend to reach maturity faster than its male counterpart. This maturity allows for easier training. This does not mean that female dogs are smarter than male dogs, of course. It just means that because they are more mature, they tend to be easier to train earlier than males of the same age. Male Australian Shepherds are also more independent than their female counterparts so try to start obedience training as soon as possible.

Aside from training, also keep the female's "heat" cycle or estrus which occurs twice a year. This is the season wherein female dogs produce a bloody vaginal secretion which attracts and lures in male dogs. The estrus lasts for around 2-3 weeks. If you do not want to breed your female dog, keep her locked inside and isolate from any male dogs during this time. Also, make sure to keep her away from carpeted floors as her bloody discharge stains. Should you have no plans of breeding your female dog, a lot of experts agree that it is best to have her spayed to lower the risk of uterine and ovarian diseases, and to lessen aggression. The best time to have her spayed is when she is about 6-9 months.

When it comes to male dogs, they tend to be more dominant and high-spirited when they are not neutered. Not only will they try to dominate other smaller dogs and animals, but they will also try to dominate you. As with their female counterparts, neuter your male dog while it is still young id you do not intend to breed him. Neutered dogs tend to be less dominant and aggressive and are less likely to roam.

Should You Choose a Purebred or Australian Shepherd Mix?

The fundamental significant difference between a purebred Australian Shepherd and an Australian Shepherd mix is that purebreds conform to a breed standard because their ancestors are all of the same breed while mixed breeds do not. From this fundamental difference, three factors are needed to be looked at when deciding on whether you should choose a purebred or mixed breed:

Predictability

Because a purebred Australian Shepherd conforms to a breed standard, you will know what you will get when you acquire one. You will know how the dog looks, what its temperament will be, how to exactly care for your pet, and how to tend to any behavioral and health issues he or she may have.

On the other hand, an Australian Shepherd mix tends to be less predictable as he or she will get some characteristics from one breed and other characteristics from another breed. How the dog will look in the future and how big he or she will be will be less predictable.

Cost

Because purebreds are bred with standards in mind, good breeders will put in a lot of effort, time and money into ensuring this. This then leads to greater costs, which then makes purebreds expensive.

On the other hand, an Australian Shepherd mix will be less expensive.

Health

Because you know what to expect with purebreds due to breed standards, you will also know what to expect when it comes to health issues associated with the dog breed. With Australian Shepherds, you will look out for genetic health conditions such as deafness or blindness in merles when purchasing a pet. You will also make sure to nurture and take care of your dog properly as to avoid particular health conditions that this breed is susceptible to such as hip dysplasia.

On the other hand, mixed breeds are said to be less prone to genetic defects and health issues; however, this does not necessarily mean that mixed breeds are healthier than purebreds.

How Much are Australian Shepherds? How Much are Australian Shepherd Puppies?

In general, Australian Shepherd puppies would cost anywhere between $200 - $2500 depending on the breeder and the dog's pedigree.

Other factors which hike up the price of an Australian Shepherd would be health clearances and other expenses that relate to top show dogs should you opt for this pedigree (includes grooming costs, handlers, etc.). On the other hand, top stockdogs usually for less.

Some breeders also demand the best quality of life for their dogs and what they spend on them usually factor in on how much their pups will be worth. They factor in the cost of alternative health care professionals, raw-fed diets, and others. On the other hand, regular breeders who do care about the dogs but do not go beyond what they require might charge a reasonably mid-range price because their dogs are not as expensive to maintain.

What Other Costs Will I Need to Account For If I Acquire an Australian Shepherd?

Owning a dog is not cheap. Make sure you take other costs into account if you are considering acquiring an Australian Shepherd.

According to the American Society for the Prevention of Cruelty to Animals (ASPCA), the costs of dog ownership exceeds $1,000 a year. Costs go beyond the initial fee you pay when you buy a dog from a breeder or adopt a dog from a shelter or rescue group.

Here are some of the costs that you need to account for:

One-time Expenses

Collar or Leash: $30

Initial Medical Exam: $70

Crate: $95 depending on size

Carrying Crate: $60

Spaying or Neutering: $200

Training: $110

Annual Expenses

License: $15

Food: $120

Toys and Treats: $55

Annual Medical Exams: $235

Pet Health Insurance: $225

Miscellaneous: $45

CHAPTER 6

Preparing Your Home for an Australian Shepherd

I f you have reached this chapter in this book, you have more likely decided on the Australian Shepherd dog breed, and are looking into where you can acquire one. However, before you take that leap, make sure you first prepare your home for your new pet. You want to make sure that your Australian Shepherd's transition from the facility he is used to your own home will be as smooth as possible.

Before you bring your Australian Shepherd home,
make sure you have all the things he or she needs.

This chapter gives you a list of the things you need to purchase before you welcome your Australian Shepherd into his new home. Also, this chapter gives particular attention as to why you need to buy a crate for your dog, and what kind of bed you should get for him or her.

The Essential Items That are a Must for Your Australian Shepherd

Before welcoming your Australian Shepherd into your family and home, make sure you have the essential items that will make him feel comfortable and nurtured. Here are some of the things you need to purchase before bringing home the newest addition to your family:

1. Food, bowls and treats.

Make sure you have plenty of food on hand, as well as bowls for food and water before you bring your Australian Shepherd home. Ask the breeder or your local veterinarian which brand and which kind of food is best for your pet. While treats are not meant to be given all the time, they are handy for when you reward your pet or when you start training him or her. With Australian Shepherds, the sooner you start training them, the better it will be for your dog and for you and your family.

2. Collar and leash.

Any dog breed will need a collar and leash for when they go outside to relieve themselves or to go for a walk. A collar and leash are especially useful when it comes to Australian Shepherds because of their intense energy. Your new dog will want to constantly exercise, run around and even dominate you. Not only will a collar and leash keep your dog safe and contained, but it will also help you train him and show him who's boss.

For walking, a 60-foot nylon or leather leash is advisable; while a 15-30-foot leash is appropriate for training sessions.

3. Microchip and ID tag.

These are extremely important as they properly identify your pet just in case he or she gets lost. While a microchip is an electronic device implanted in your dog which gives him or her a unique number, his collar should have an ID tag that shows your dog's name as well as your contact information.

4. Grooming materials and tools.

From toothbrushes to toothpaste, to brushes and shampoos made specifically for dogs, these grooming materials and tools keep your Australian Shepherd clean and healthy. Australian Shepherds have mid-length fur and they do tend to shed. Make sure you keep your dog's coat and overall body clean and healthy.

5. First aid kit.

Accidents happen, especially if you own the highly energetic and adventurous Australian Shepherd. As a responsible dog owner, make sure that you have a first aid kit for your pet which includes a cold compress, bandage and antiseptic skin ointment. Also make sure that you have your vet's number on hand should you need his or her advice, and bring your pet immediately to the vet in cases of emergency.

6. Dog toys.

Not only do dog toys keep your Australian Shepherd entertained and busy, but these also keep him or her out of trouble and mischief. Make sure the toys you choose are safe for your dog. Australian Shepherds love Frisbees, balls and other toys that they can integrate into their activities and exercise.

7. Cleaning supplies.

Make sure you have cleaning supplies on hand before you bring your pet home. Dogs make a lot of mess, especially when they are still puppies. Buy cleaning supplies that not only disinfect but also removes stains and smells.

8. Crate.

The crate will make your Australian Shepherd feel safe and comfortable, especially since your home will be a totally new environment for your new pet. The value of the crate will be further discussed in the next section.

The Value of the Dog Crate for Your Australian Shepherd

As mentioned previously, a dog crate will make your pet feel safe and comfortable, especially during his first night in your home. The crate is also an effective tool to use when you want to housetrain your puppy. However, remember to never use the crate as punishment. Never leave your dog, especially if you own an Australian Shepherd, inside the dog crate for extended periods. Doing this is simply cruel.

Crate training will give your dog a sense of security and safety.

Here are some other things that you need to remember about dog crates:

1. Buy a dog crate that is big enough for your pet to at least turn around in. It should not feel cramped.

2. Place the crate where the dog feels comfortable in and doesn't cause him or her further stress.

3. Create a positive association with the crate and training. You can do this by giving him or her treats or even feeding him or her inside or near the crate. However, make sure to remove the feeding bowls from the crate as soon as possible.

4. Dogs will naturally try to avoid relieving themselves where they eat and sleep. It is your responsibility to give your pet the opportunity to relieve himself or herself outside as soon as he or she needs to.

5. Successful crate training depends on being consistent and positive. Make sure to give your pet a routine and to lavish him or her with praise when he or she can follow your training and instructions properly.

Choosing Toys for Australian Shepherd

Remember that dog toys are not luxury items. They are necessary. Not only do they provide entertainment to your canine companion, but toys also help prevent boredom and problem behaviors and aid in giving comfort. Toys can also be used to train puppies and younger dogs. Also, dogs tend to be orally fixated, so they can utilize toys to satisfy this instinct and learn about the world.

When choosing a dog toy, there are several things you need to consider such as:

1. **The size of your dog.** Choose toys that are large enough that he or she won't swallow them. Your dog will likely bite, chew and try to tear the toy apart make sure the toy you buy isn't too small that it is able to find its way to your dog's throat. Instead, large rubber toys are more ideal for big dogs because they are harder to swallow and chew.

2. **How active your dog is.** The way your dog plays will change as he or she ages. Remember that a teething puppy will be more active than an elderly dog, and will more likely enjoy toys that he or she can run around with.

3. **Your dog's play style.** Some dogs like playing tug-of-war while others prefer running around with a ball or chewing a squeaky toy. Buy toys your dog will enjoy playing with.

4. **His or her environment.** The type of toy you choose for your pet will also depend on your home. For example, if you live in an apartment and have no access to a park, you wouldn't really have much use for a Frisbee.

When choosing toys for your Australian Shepherd, always consider that this dog breed is extremely intelligent, athletic, hardworking and energetic. Make sure to choose toys that are geared towards dogs that have an active lifestyle, rather than toys that aren't much good for anything other than chewing.

Some of the best toys for Australian Shepherds include balls, Frisbees and discs because these are easily integrated into his exercise and physical activities. On the other hand, toys which stimulate this dog's smarts such as certain puzzle are also good for this breed. While the Australian Shepherd could still potentially appreciate a good chew toy, he or she will easily get bored with it or may even opt to destroy it.

While there are different toys you can opt for your Australian Shepherd, make sure that you purchase safe ones. When choosing toys for your dog, here are some of the unsafe ones you should avoid:

1. Toys with hazardous materials and embellishments such as string, ribbons, rubber bands, small plastic eyes and feathers. These are choking hazards and can cause an intestinal obstruction when ingested.
2. Children's toys and pantyhose.
3. Tennis balls are hazardous to large breeds with larger mouths.

Australian Shepherd Bible and the Australian Shepherd

Also, small rubber balls are also dangerous as they can become slimy when chewed on and can easily slip down your dog's throat.

4. Toys that contain toxins such as carcinogenic agents, poisons, dyes and preservatives, heavy metals, stain guard, fire retardants, and some latex. Do a sniff test on the toy to check for these toxins. Those with strong chemical smells will have residual chemicals that may be highly toxic to your dog.

5. Toys made of soft plastics as your dog can ingest them.

6. Toys with sharp parts and corners.

7. Although some owners do give them to their dogs to play with, never give your pet rib and poultry bones as they may break and splinter and cause a blockage in the throat. These can also cause the teeth of your pet to chip.

8. Pig ears and bone marrow. These can cause intestinal distress.

CHAPTER 7

Bringing Home Your Australian Shepherd

When introducing your Australian Shepherd to his or her new home, remember that while you may be comfortable in your environment, it is a new and unfamiliar place for your new family member. Take things slowly, especially on his or her first day.

Be patient and give your dog time to adjust, especially during his or her first night.

Here are some tips to consider when introducing your Australian Shepherd to his or her new home:

1. Give your dog the time to adjust.

Your Australian Shepherd is more likely feeling uneasy, insecure and frightened by the change of environment. Not only will he or she be feeling homesick, but he or she will also be missing his or her mother and siblings. Show your new pet where his crate or bed is, as well as where you put his food and water bowls. Take him or her outside when he or she needs to relieve himself or herself. Allow your pet to explore his or her surroundings. Do not pressure your new family member to feel comfortable right away. Supervise him or her, and give your Australian Shepherd the time to adjust.

2. Introduce your pet to other members of your household, which includes other pets if you have any.

Slowly introduce your new pet to other members of the household. Do not allow everyone to pet him or her all at once as this may overwhelm and frighten him or her. If you have children, teach them how to properly pet and interact with your new dog. Socialization is important for your Australian Shepherd's development, but make sure to do this properly and slowly.

Your other pets should also be correctly introduced to your Australian Shepherd. Remember that Australian Shepherds have a tendency of herding or even becoming aggressive towards other dogs and animals. While you shouldn't expect them to play together right away, make sure to socialize them slowly so that they are able to adjust to one another and get along as time progresses.

3. Train your dog.

Though your new Australian Shepherd may be new to your household and even if the Australian Shepherd you opt for is a puppy, train your new pet as soon as he has adjusted. House training is particularly important so he or she knows where to go to relieve himself or herself right away. Accidents do happen but consistent housetraining will make it easier for you and will set a routine for your pet.

4. Enforce rules and be the boss.

Australian Shepherds tend to be dominant dogs, so your pet will more likely try to be the alpha dog of your pack. From the start, make sure to teach your new pet what is appropriate and what is not. Enforce the house rules and be consistent. Remember that a well-behaved Australian Shepherd is the result of consistent training.

Your Australian Shepherd's First Night

Do note that your puppy is more likely to cry and whine during his first night. After all, it will be the first night he or she will be spending with you and away from his mother and siblings. Because dogs are pack animals, he or she instinctively knows that being away from his or her pack is dangerous. Crying and whining are his or her way of calling for his pack to find him or her. Be there for your new pet. Comfort him or her. Do not lose your patience with your dog or force him or her to adjust right away as this may just make your Australian Shepherd even more fearful and nervous.

Your Australian Shepherds' first night in his new home will be difficult for your pet and for yourself. Make sure to stay with your new pet during his first night. Not only will this make him or her feel more comfortable, but he or she will also feel more bonded with you. You may either sleep on the couch in his or her area, or you may even opt to place your dog's crate next to your bed.

Before going to bed, spend some time playing and bonding with your new Australian Shepherd puppy. Tire him or her out so that he or she will get tired enough that he or she sleeps soundly. Do not let your new pet nap within an hour or so before bedtime or else he or she will be up all night.

Also, bring your puppy to his soiling area before going to sleep. Praise your new pet and bring him back to where he is to sleep. This not only lessens the number of trips to the loo you need to make with your new pet when he or she needs to relieve himself or herself during the night, and it helps you start house training from the get-go.

While you cannot expect to get a good night's sleep for at least a week, this builds trust in your pet and it will help him or her adjust to his or her new home. Be patient with your new family member.

House Training Your Australian Shepherd

While it is best to house train your pet as soon as possible, also make sure that you do not rush it. Keep in mind that training your Australian Shepherd will take some time. Rushing will only lead to frustration and possibly anger. You don't want that, and your dog does not need that. Your dog will benefit from successful house training if you are patient. After all, whatever your dog learns, he will learn from you. Be patient. Be consistent. And remember to always be loving towards your Australian Shepherd.

Here are some important things to remember when house training your Australian Shepherd:

Consistency is key to successful training.

1. Remember that your Australian Shepherd has a den instinct.

As previously mentioned, your pet will typically not relieve himself where he eats and sleeps. This is referred to as his "den instinct".

You can take advantage of your Australian Shepherd's den instinct by first making his or her world a smaller place. While your whole house may be your "den" (minus your toilet, of course), your house is a huge place where he or she can find a lot of good spots to relieve himself or herself. Enclose your puppy in a smaller area where you would want him or her to eat, sleep and play. Preferably having easy-to-clean flooring, place sheets of newspaper in one part of the area and designate it as your dog's bathroom. Encourage your pup to relieve himself there. A good tip to remember is when you clean up the newspapers, leave a sheet or two since the urine scent left on them will entice your dog to relieve himself or herself in this area again next time.

Remember that while this is the first step to house training your Australian Shepherd, you should gradually train him or her to relieve himself or herself outside.

2. Pay close attention to your puppy most of the time.

This will involve knowing when your pet has eaten or drank, whether he or she has been playing or just woken up from a nap. These are times that your Australian Shepherd will more likely want to relieve himself or herself. When this occurs, take your dog outside so he can do a poo or a wee. While others remember to bring their pet to the same spot consistently, a good tip to remember is to take the same path to the spot as well at all times. This will help your pet associate doing a poo or a wee with the path as well as the spot.

Aside from associating the spot and the path with relieving himself or herself, your dog can be further trained with your chosen command word or phrase to signal a poo or wee. Repeat this every time you bring your Australian Shepherd outside so he or she can relieve himself or herself. This dog breed is a smart one, and this will help your pet to quickly associate the spot, path and command with successful completion of his or her task. Be sure to praise your pet when he or she is successful.

3. Consistency is key to success when it comes to house training.

For human beings, repetition is the best way for us to truly learn. The same goes with dogs. Be consistent especially when it comes to Australian Shepherds. Australian Shepherds are smart, but they will want to dominate you. This need to be the alpha dog will also mean that your pet will also try to be the boss. Make sure you are consistent with your training so that your dog not only learns what you teach him or her, but he or she also gets to understand that you are the leader of the pack.

4. Don't punish your dog when he is not successful.

House training requires a lot of energy, time and patience. When your dog makes a mistake, or does not follow your lead, do not yell. Do not be impatient. And most importantly, do not hit your pet.

If you show anger and frustration, your pet will associate house training with your negativity and it will only lead to setbacks. Your dog will also more likely hide from you because he or she will associate house training with fear and anxiety.

Instead of being angry or frustrated, be stern and firm when you see your pet misbehaving or doing something undesirable inside the house. Bring your dog outside when he or she needs to poo or wee, forget about the mistake he made, and make sure to lavish him or her with praise when he or she does his business.

CHAPTER 8

Caring for Your Australian Shepherd

U pon acquiring your Australian Shepherd, you made a commitment to not only provide shelter for your dog, but to welcome him or her into your family and to care for him. Australian Shepherds could be challenging to take care of, but the great thing is, they are easy to love.

Owning an Australian Shepherd can be challenging but the great news is they are easy to love!

This chapter gives you tips regarding how to properly exercise your Australian Shepherd so that he or she not only stays healthy, but so that he or she is productive instead of destructive. Also, this chapter gives you tips on how to groom your Australian Shepherd, with particular attention to choosing the right brush for your dog. After all, you want your Australian Shepherd looking his or her best especially since his or her coat is one of the most striking things about him or her.

Properly Exercising Your Australian Shepherd

As was mentioned time and time again, Australian Shepherds thrive on exercise. They like being active and working hard, and become destructive, bored and restless when they have nothing to do. When they have no activities, and are not engaged in activities they can gain a whole lot of weight and become lethargic. This is unhealthy for most dogs, but most especially for the usually spirited and highly energetic Australian Shepherd.

They constantly desire to interact and engage with their owners and families, making them ideal exercise and activity partners for adventurous and active people. Because they can bond intensely and want to constantly be around their owners, they do not tend to wander off too far if you decide to take them with you when you ski, bike, climb, hike, run or others.

*Your Australian Shepherd thrives on daily
exercise and desires constant interaction.*

Remember that Australian Shepherd puppies do not need strenuous exercise as much as adult dogs do. Generally, adult Australian Shepherds need around 30-60 minutes of exercise daily, and prefer high-energy activities such as playing with a Frisbee. This dog breed also thrives when given a job to do such as herding, doing search and rescue, getting involved in obedience training and others. While these dogs typically love running around wide open spaces, they will still be able to thrive in backyards as long as there is enough space to run and play.

Here are some of the activities and sports you can involve your Australian Shepherd with:

1. **Herding.** Bred to be stockdogs, your Australian Shepherd thrives when herding other animals in the farm.

2. **Frisbee or Disc.** A sport dominated by the highly energetic and athletic Australian Shepherd, this dog breed loves getting involved with it because it showcases his jumping and fetching ability, speed and agility.

3. **Agility Training.** Activities that are involved with training such as obstacle courses not only provides the Australian Shepherd with exercise but with mental stimulation as well.

4. **Obedience Training.** Not only does this challenge and exercise both your dog's physicality and mental prowess, but it also helps establish you as the leader of the pack.

5. **Tracking.** The Australian Shepherd can not only showcase his scent trailing ability, but he or she thrives in the socialization involved in this activity.

6. **Search and Rescue.** A good number of Australian Shepherds are involved with disaster-relief organizations. The breed is also good when it comes to policing.

7. **Flyball.** This activity is one that Australian Shepherds find enjoyable since it involves going through hurdles and fetching with a team.

8. **Therapy.** Because Australian Shepherds thrive when socializing and because they are meant to have gentle temperaments, this dog is a go-to breed when it comes to lifting the spirits of people in hospitals and elder care facilities. Not only are they great dogs to play with, but they also love receiving cuddles.

Australian Shepherd Brush Types

The Australian Shepherd dog breed loves the outdoors. Because of this love for the outdoors, they are prone to picking up debris, dirt, leaves, grasses and twigs on their fur. This necessitates regular grooming.

Choose a brush type that suits your dog's plush, double-layered fur.

If you are wondering what type of brush you should purchase for your Australian Shepherd, keep their fur in mind. Not only do a good number of Australian Shepherds have striking merle patterns, but also their mid-length coats are plush and double-layered. The reason that their coats are plush and double-layered is that they needed protection from extreme climates. But also, because the dog's coat is double-layered, it is best to keep it properly groomed always. The outer hairs require different care from the inner soft and fluffy undercoat; therefore, different types of brushes should be used if you want your dog's coat to be as best as it can be.

Groom your dog every day and remove tangles before they become knots with the following brushes:

1. Slicker brush

One of the best brushes to purchase for your Australian Shepherd is a slicker brush.

A slicker brush is a flat, paddle-like brush containing a lot of fire wires. It is stroked over the coat of your Australian Shepherd following the direction of his or her hairs. The fine wires grasp loose hair and aid in their removal. This brush can also be used if you want to lift out and remove tangles and small knots.

While the fine wires are certainly effective at removing loose hairs and detangling, they tend to also scratch and irritate the dog's skin if you put too much pressure on the brush.

The slicker brush is an excellent option to choose because when your dog sheds its undercoat, hairs can get trapped and tangled in the long outer coat. This then results in a coat that is susceptible to tangling and looks messy and dull.

Use a slicker brush on your Australian Shepherd at least once a week; although, it is recommended that you use the brush as often as possible. Remember to use gentle pressure when using this brush so you do not end up hurting your Australian Shepherd.

2. Pin brush

The great thing about the pin brush is that the tips of the pins are rounded; thus, they don't scratch and irritate the skin of your Australian Shepherd like the wires of the slicker brush. The said pins are also mounted on a soft rubber cushion which allows some "give" and prevents you from placing too much pressure on the brush when you use it. Instead, the brush is able to comfort to the contours of the Australian Shepherd's body.

The pin brush is great at penetrating the coat and realigning the hairs while lifting away loose hairs. It leaves the coat smooth and shiny.

The disadvantage of this brush is that because the pins are anchored to the rubber cushion, they either become loose or dislodged over time.

3. Rubber grooming brush

This type of brush is very gentle on the skin because it has not sharp metal pins which can irritate and scratch. The rubber grooming brush is, therefore, a good introduction grooming tool to use on Australian Shepherd puppies. Giving dogs a sensation of being stroked and massaged, this brush teaches puppies to relax and enjoy when brushed and groomed.

Another advantage of the rubber grooming brush is that the dragging movement that it makes helps spread natural oils over the coat, which then results in fur that looks shiner and healthier. Also, this brush can be used on either a wet or dry coat.

The unfortunate aspect about this brush, however, is that it can't really remove tangles from a long coat.

4. Comb

Combs are essential tools when it comes to grooming. They are necessary for Australian Shepherds because they have longer outer coats. Combs keep your Australian Shepherd's coat free from tangles as it can separate hair strands. After using a comb, utilize a brush to smooth the surface of the coat down.

These can also be used to detangle knots in parts of your dog's body where hair strands rub against other strands, namely behind the airs, between back legs and in the armpits.

It is recommended that you purchase two combs (one large and one small) that have different gauge halves. These two varieties well help you work on smaller and tighter areas of your dog's body, as well as larger areas.

5. De-shedding brush

While Australian Shepherds do not shed as much as other breeds, they still do shed. Make sure you purchase a de-shedding brush. Not only will this tool keep your dog's coat from loose hair, but using it regularly will also lessen the number of fur balls you find in your house.

Remember that if not used properly, a de-shedding brush can hurt your Australian Shepherd. Make sure to draw the blade of the brush gently over the surface of the coat and allow the brush to do the work rather than applying too much pressure on it.

Grooming Australian Shepherds

When it comes to grooming your Australian Shepherd, there are certain processes you need to do to make sure that your pet is as clean, healthy and well-maintained as possible.

Grooming involves the following:

Bathing

Bathing your Australian Shepherd can be challenging in the beginning; however, with proper preparation, positivity and perseverance, bathing will not only help your dog stay clean and healthy, but it will also become both fun and fulfilling.

Because your Australian Shepherd has a combination, double-layered coat, your pet needs to be bathed seasonally or about every three months at a minimum. However, it is advisable that you do it more often than that, especially when your pet needs it; and with the adventurous, active Australian Shepherd, he or she will certainly need it.

Before bathing, make sure to give your pet a good brushing to remove mats and loose hair. You can either bathe your Australian Shepherd in a tub inside the house with lukewarm water, or outside with a spray hose or pitcher. Remember to be careful not to get water in your dog's eyes, nose and ears.

Massage in the dog shampoo into your dog's body, leaving his or her head for last. Immediately rinse the shampoo thoroughly, making sure that you don't leave any residue. Towel dry your

Australian Shepherd. After bathing, your Australian Shepherd should smell fresh and be free of shedding or loose hair.

Brushing the coat

Brushing is done before bathing when the coat of your dog is matted or tangled, and after bathing. No other part of grooming typically requires as much time or commitment as brushing. Don't forget this part of the process as routine brushing not only keeps your Australian Shepherd's coat clean and free of tangles and knots, it also keeps his or her skin's health as it distributes his or her natural oils, removes loose fur and stimulates blood flow.

Because Australian Shepherds have double-layered coats, they are prone to having mats and tangles. They also experience seasonal shedding. As mentioned previously, use the proper brushes when grooming your Australian Shepherd. Slicker brushes and pin brushes are particularly vital when it comes to removing mats and tangles, while keeping your pet's coat smooth and shiny. Pay particular attention to the fur around and under your Australian Shepherd's neck and hind legs. If your pet's coat contains stubborn mats, tangles and knots, opt to use baby oil or a liquid de-tangler. Gently massage the baby oil or liquid de-tangler on the difficult areas and brush to help remove and loosen the hairs.

While Australian Shepherds do not shed as much as other breeds, their coats look their best if you routinely brush them and will help keep their shedding under control. If you are not able to brush your pet every day, try to do it at least once per week.

Cleaning sensitive areas and trimming hair around it

While not all dog breeds require regular trimming around their eyes and ears, owners are advised to inspect these sensitive areas on a regular basis. These areas tend to accumulate gunk and are therefore more susceptible to infections.

If your Australian Shepherd's ears need cleaning, moisten a cotton ball with a store-bought ear cleaning solution, mineral oil, olive oil or witch hazel. Gently wipe the ear, making sure that you avoid the ear canal. Remember never to use a cotton bud as it can damage the dog's inner ear if he or she moves while you are cleaning.

On the other hand, dogs can develop tear stains around the eyes which may cause infection and affect their vision if left unattended. Use a cotton ball or soft cloth with a tear stain solution to remove the stains and a small trimmer to trim excess hair.

Cutting nails

A good number of pet owners are anxious about cutting and trimming their dogs' nails thinking they might cut too quick and hurt them. However, nail clipping can be simple and stress free with the right conditioning and tools and cautious cutting.

Before cutting your Australian Shepherd's nails, make sure that he or she associates this process with positivity. Use treats to make this step pleasant for him or her. As you begin clipping his or her nails, gently press on his or her paws so your pet gets used to the feeling of getting his or her nails trimmed. Work gradually and bit-by-bit to make sure that you don't trim too much. Clip one nail and reward your Australian Shepherd with a treat. Lavish him or her with praise when he or she remains still and allows you to trim his or her nails.

A tip to remember so that you don't cut too much off is that his or her nails become softer as you get closer to the paw. This is the reason for gradual cutting as well – so that once you feel that the nail is softer, it means that you should stop as you are getting closer to his skin.

Hair cut or hair trim

This process is actually a lot easier than you think, especially if you have the proper clipper, trimmer and scissors on hand. If you have the right tools, you don't even have to pay a groomer to do this if you simply need to give your pet a simple trim.

Because your Australian Shepherd has a double-layered coat, he will require regular trimming and stripping. This dog breed tends to attract fleas and other pests, get dirt and other debris on his or her coat, and is susceptible to tangles and mats due to his penchant for heavy activity and the outdoors. Regular trimming not only reduces loose hairs, shedding and tangles, it also reduces the risk of skin infection.

There is no general rule when it comes to the frequency of hair trimming; rather, judge for yourself if you think your dog needs it. Remember though that it will do you and your Australian Shepherd good if you take him or her out for a short walk to calm him or her down before you trim his or her coat.

When cutting his or her hair, use trimmers to remove the excess fur off of his or her body first. Begin with his or her shoulders and progress towards the tail. Don't forget to even out the areas around his tail, paws, tummy and chest if needed. Take extra care when grooming his head and face, and remember to trim with the flow of the fur.

Brushing teeth

Because many consider "doggy breath" as normal, they tend to forget to brush their pets' teeth regularly. However, remember that some dogs are prone to dental problems such as cavities, gum disease, tartar buildup and sensitive teeth. Combat these issues with frequent brushing. Make sure to use a toothbrush and toothpaste made especially for dogs. Brush your dog's teeth at least once a week – more if possible.

CHAPTER 9

Feeding Your Australian Shepherd

L ike any other dog breed (or creature, for that matter), diet is extremely important for the Australian Shepherd to not only survive but to thrive.

This chapter will teach you what to consider when it comes to the nutritional needs of your Australian Shepherd, and will guide you on choosing the right dog food for your beloved pet.

The Value of the Nutritional Needs of Australian Shepherds – What is Important to Consider?

While some pet owners opt to feed their dogs whatever dog food they first see in the pet store, or table scraps, Australian Shepherds have particular dietary needs that need to be considered. If you want your Australian Shepherd to be in his or her optimal health for as long as possible, always keep the following in mind:

Your Australian Shepherd's Nutritional Needs

Puppies and working dogs burn more calories,
therefore they need more food.

According to the National Research Council of the National Academies, a typical active adult Australian Shepherd weighing 50 pounds requires an average daily caloric intake of 1353 calories. Older dogs or dogs that have been neutered or spayed usually need fewer calories than mentioned this is because more active dogs tend to need more calories depending on their level of activity. Growing puppies and working dogs usually burn more calories and therefore need more food to burn.

Like with other dog breeds, Australian Shepherds need good quality protein. According to the Association of American Feed Control Officials (AAFCO), puppies require a minimum of 22% protein in their diets, while adult dogs require 18%.

Fat is also an important source of energy for Australian Shepherds and should make up 8% of the diet of puppies and 5% of the diet of adult dogs. Not only is fat important to a dog's diet, but it also adds flavor to food and makes it more appealing to your pet. Fat is also a source of vital fatty acids (such as omega-3 and omega-6) which are beneficial to your dog's skin, coat, brain and heart.

Your Australian Shepherd's Special Health Issues

Like any other dog breed, the Australian Shepherd can suffer from particular health issues, including elbow dysplasia, hip dysplasia, cancer, thyroid disease and epilepsy. Your Australian Shepherd's health issues will be further discussed later in the book.

Remember that your Australian Shepherd's health could potentially be affected by his or her diet. Keeping an eye on your Australian Shepherd's diet could potentially prevent your pet from suffering from these health issues.

Hip or elbow dysplasia

Like other medium and large dog breeds, Australian Shepherds can suffer from hip or elbow dysplasia. These conditions are usually brought about by excess weight. Dogs that are overweight or obese aggravate dysplasia and arthritis, especially when they become older. This is because extra weight adds extra stress on your pet's joints and bones.

The fortunate aspect of Australian Shepherds is that they thrive when doing physical activities, so you are unlikely to worry about them becoming overweight not unless you do ignore their need for exercise. However, these dogs can pack on the extra pounds as they get older and their metabolism changes. As they get older, you may need to adjust your pet's diet.

We also advise that you measure the amount of food you feed your dog. If you have more than one dog, keep an eye on how they eat. You may need to feed them separately so that they eat at their own pace because dogs eating right next to each other tend to get influenced by their companions when it comes to speed of eating.

Cancer

Like with other dog breeds, Australian Shepherds can suffer from cancer. While it is difficult to predict and prevent cancer from occurring, breeders and professionals suggest feeding your pet dog feed that is free of artificial colors, sweeteners, preservatives and other questionable ingredients that have been brought up in various studies.

Hyperthyroidism

This health condition can occur in Australian Shepherds. Symptoms of hyperthyroidism include rapid weight gain, hair loss and lethargy. This won't be related to food intake as your pet will have to consume an extreme amount of ingredient that contains iodine to affect his or her thyroid levels.

If you think your pet may have hyperthyroidism, consult with your vet. The fortunate thing is that once the thyroid problem has been identified, it is easily treated. Make sure that if your dog has a thyroid problem, soy and other ingredients sometimes found in dog food may interfere with the medication he or she will need to take.

Epilepsy

Your Australian Shepherd can also be afflicted with epilepsy. Unfortunately, there are no DNA tests now to show if a dog is prone to this illness, and causes are not completely understood yet. However, in some cases, it is believed that ingredients such as monosodium glutamate (MSG) and rosemary can trigger a seizure. Like allergies, individual dogs can have their own personal food triggers; make sure you observe your pet and try to avoid food or ingredients which may cause a seizure.

How do I choose the right dog food for my Australian Shepherd?

Because there are tons of dog food brands out there, choosing the best one for your Australian Shepherd can be confusing and even overwhelming. Dog food brands can be dependent on your own preference, the referrals of others and the cost of the products. However, while it is really up to you as a dog owner to choose which brand will be best for your dog, here are the specific ingredients you need to look for when buying dog food:

The right dog food contains protein, fat, DHA and proper ratio of calcium to phosphorus.

Protein

Like all other dog breeds, Australian Shepherds need good quality protein in their diet. It is important that you not only opt for protein, but for good quality ones because even if you are giving your pet a whole lot of protein, if it is not from a good quality source, your Australian Shepherd's body won't be able to utilize it properly.

While the brand of dog food you opt for will be dependent on your preference, remember that ideally, it should feature meat proteins in the first few ingredients instead of grain or some other form of carbohydrate. When meats are lower on the ingredients list, it means that water from the meats was removed, which is not desirable.

Remember that the term "whole meats" refer to whole chicken, fish, beef or lamb. This is a term you want to see in the dog food you buy. Less desirable terms when it comes to meat are "digests" and "by-products".

Fat

While fat is not a term that usually connotes, dogs do need fat from good sources. Your dog will be needing some vitamins which they can only digest with fat. Some of the fat sources and terms you should remember when choosing food for your Australian Shepherd are "chicken fat" and "fish oil" which provides your pet with essential omega-3 fatty acids that keep his or her coat shiny and skin healthy.

Docosahexaenoic Acid (DHA)

Docosahexaenoic acid (DHA) is a compound found in puppy food. While tips for feeding puppies and adults dogs are similar, DHA is necessary for puppies (and even human children) as this helps with their brain development.

Proper Ratio of Calcium to Phosphorus

The food you give your Australian Shepherd puppy has to have the proper ratio of calcium to phosphorus. It is recommended that puppy food contains the ratio of 1.2 parts of calcium for each 1 part of phosphorous. Remember, however, that if you add other food to your puppy's diet such as cheese, yogurt or milk, it will disturb this ratio and may lead to health issues in the future. It is then vital that you not give too many supplements to your puppy in his first year of life, not unless the vet advises you to do so.

Avoid dog food that has artificial preservatives such as BHT, BHA, and ethoxyquin, as well as colorings, sweeteners and artificial flavors. Not only does your Australian Shepherd not need these, but these ingredients could also possibly be related to the development of cancer.

Also, nutritionists encourage avoiding dog food that is grain-free, because while protein is a vital addition to your Australian Shepherd's diet, dog food that are grain-free tend to have too much protein, too much fat, calories and the ration of calcium to phosphorus are usually off. This disparity makes dogs grow too big too soon. The rapid growth then leads to joint and bone problems.

To make sure that your Australian Shepherd is getting the necessary nutrition, they should not be allowed to become roly-poly. You should still be able to feel their ribs, but you are not supposed to see them protruding. For all dog breeds, exercise is good. For Australian Shepherds, exercise is absolutely necessary.

CHAPTER 10

Australian Shepherd Training for Beginners

Aside from proper diet, Australian Shepherds need proper training to thrive. Not only does proper training help keep your pet mentally stimulated, but it also helps ensure that your Australian Shepherd is well-behaved and well-socialized.

Because Australian Shepherds are dominant dogs,
training them can be challenging.

This chapter teaches you how to train your Australian Shepherd with basic commands such as "sit" and "stay". You will also learn how to crate train your dog to keep your pet secure and comfortable, as well helping him or her become housetrained.

How to Train Australian Shepherds

Australian Shepherds are highly intelligent and energetic but, they are also very dominant dogs. This is not surprising as these dogs were raised to dominate and herd stock animals. Because of this dominant characteristic, Australian Shepherds need to be trained as soon as possible. Expect to have a power struggle with your dog as he or she will try to be the alpha dog of your pack.

Here are some of the things to consider when training your Australian Shepherd:

1. Socialize your pet as soon as you bring him or her home.

It is important that your pet not only gets used to you but that he or she gets used to other members of the family and other pets in your home. Allow him or her to get used to other people, other places and other animals. When an Australian Shepherd is not socialized early, he or she is likely to be anxious and fearful of others and may end up with behavior problems such as fear biting. On the other hand, a socialized dog can behave well and take on instructions from his or her owners properly.

2. Housebreak your Australian Shepherd as early as possible.

Your dog will want to keep where he sleeps and eats clean; however, he or she may designate pooing and weeing spots inside the house. Make sure to crate train your dog, keeping him or her inside the crate to relieve himself; and then eventually, teach him or her how to poo or wee outside. Be patient and don't get frustrated or angry. Reward your pet and lavish him or her with praise when he or she relieves himself or herself in the right spot.

3. Teach basic obedience early.

As mentioned previously, Australian Shepherds are dominant dogs; therefore, it is imperative that you teach your pet basic obedience as early as possible so you have some control over him or her from the get-go. Join a training class and follow through with this training at home. If you are not headstrong and do not show leadership, your Australian Shepherd will not listen to you and will misbehave.

4. Get your Australian Shepherd involved in a sport or regular play.

This dog breed excels in activities such as herding, agility, rally and obedience training. Not only do these activities give him the opportunity to exercise and expend his energy, they give your pet a purpose. A purpose is extremely important for this hardworking breed.

If it is something you are interested in, you and your Australian Shepherd may even compete together in events. Not only will getting involved in these get you and your pet exercising, but it will also strengthen your bond.

Australian Shepherd Training - How to Sit

Of all the basic commands, "sit" is the easiest to teach your dog.

The sit command is one of the fundamentals of obedience training, and one of the easiest to do. The key to your dog mastering this trick is consistency on your end. So how do you teach your Australian Shepherd to sit? Through the following steps:

1. Find a quiet spot to train your Australian Shepherd.

Australian Shepherds, especially puppies, are balls of energy. To get your pet's full attention and focus, do your training in a quiet spot where there are not distractions. If you have children or other pets at home, keep them away while training your Australian Shepherd.

2. Put his or her leash on and tell him to sit.

Say the word "sit" in a calm, firm tone. Do not be aggressive as this will just teach your Australian Shepherd to be afraid of you. Say "sit" again, only this time, gently push down on his or her backside. After he or she sits down with your assistance, lavish him or her with praise and give him or her a treat. Remember to give the treat after he has spent a few seconds sitting. If your Australian Shepherd jumps up immediately, pull the treat away. The reason for this is you want your pet to know what he or she is being rewarded for.

3. Repeat.

Repetition is key. You may need to push on your Australian Shepherd's backside before he understands your command; but because this dog breed is highly intelligent, this will not take long. Make sure you consistently praise your dog and give him or her treats for a job well done.

Australian Shepherd Training - Calling Your Australian Shepherd with a Whistle

Use a sheepdog whistle to call and train your Australian Shepherd.

Australian Shepherds respond particularly well to training with a sheepdog whistle. The said whistle is held against your tongue as you blow. The sound that is the produced through the top and bottom holes and then out from the slit between the two flat sides referred to as the "sound chamber". The great feature of the whistle is that aside from being able to utilize this tool to train your dog to follow several specific commands (such as "Stop" or to call him or her to come back), it allows you to communicate with your pet from a great distance.

Here is how you can use a whistle to call your Australian Shepherd:

1. Make sure to hold the whistle by its tab.

2. Place the whistle in your mouth, making sure that the tab is at the front and the closed end in against the tongue. Do not block the openings as these will be releasing the sound. Make sure air is going through the hole on top and bottom and the slits between the flat sides when you blow.

3. While taking care not to block the slot, seal the edges of the whistle with your lips. Use your tongue to push the whistle in the right position, making sure that it does not sit flat on the tongue. Make sure your tongue is below the whistle so the air can circulate.

4. Breathe from your chest.

5. You can change the tone of the whistle by using your tongue to vary the direction of the air you are breathing out. Begin with one single consistent tone as practice. Eventually, you will be able to master this tool and you will be able to create more tones.

Australian Shepherd Training - How to Stay

While sitting still is a huge challenge for a good number of dogs, it is especially challenging for the energetic Australian Shepherd dog or puppy. Before you train your dog how to stay, make sure that he or she has already mastered the sit or lie down commands. To train your pet to stay, start small until your dog gets it right, then gradually get to more advanced training. For an energetic dog, this will mean half-second stays; from half-second stays, progress to longer.

Train your Australian Shepherd with the following steps:

1. Do your training in a familiar area with your dog, but make sure that there are no distractions around such as noise, children and other pets. Make sure your dog is focused.

2. Stand in front of him or her and look your pet in the eye. Hold a treat in your hand and ask your dog to sit or lie down. If your dog holds his or her position for a few seconds, give him or her the treat.

3. Do the same sit or lie down command, making your Australian Shepherd hold the position for a few seconds longer. If he or she manages to do this, give another treat. Repeat this for a few more times.

4. Once your dog is responding how you would like him or her to, add another verbal cue. Ask your dog to sit or lie down, then say "stay" while holding your hand out with your palm toward her nose as if saying "stop". If your pet holds the position for a second or two, lavish him or her with praise and give him or her a treat. Repeat this step, gradually asking your Australian Shepherd to stay a second longer than the last successful attempt.

5. If this command does not work and your dog breaks the command, say "sit" or "lie down" depending on which position your dog was originally in. Try the stay command again.

If you want to make the stay command more challenging, you can progress to a more advanced command once your Australian Shepherd has mastered the basic training. You can do this through by doing the following steps:

1. Stand a foot away from your Australian Shepherd and ask your pet to stay. Gradually increase your distance every time your dog successfully follows your command.

2. Turn your back from your pet and ask him or her to stay. Gradually increase your distance every time your dog successfully follows your command.

3. Do the same thing when there is a distraction around – a dog toy, dog kibble, ball bouncing, another person or dog in the distance.

Australian Shepherd Training – Go to Crate Command and Your Australian Shepherd

Crate training is a vital part of housetraining your Australian Shepherd. Not only does crate training help your pet to feel secure and comfortable, it also helps in aiding your pet to get housetrained.

When used properly, a crate is a great short-term tool to manage and train your dog. It is especially useful and effective when you are introducing your dog to his new home, and prevent him or her from being destructive.

While crates are effective tools, they can also be misused. Remember that crates are not housing. They are not meant to be used to house your dog for his lifetime. The goal is to work on his or her behavioral issues through the crate instead of utilizing it is to keep him or her contained and confined 8-10 hours or even more every day.

Remember that different dogs react in various ways to crates. Some don't like it but tolerate it, while others panic when placed inside. However, the majority of dogs do readily adjust to crates and even prefer to take refuge inside it when things outside get too tiring or stressful.

Crate training can take anywhere from a few days to a few weeks, depending on how your dog accepts the training, his or her age, temperament and history. But while this is certainly true, it is important to take these two things in mind always: (1) Crate training should be a positive experience; (2) Do not rush.

You can teach your Australian Shepherd the crate command through the following steps:

1. Introduce your Australian Shepherd to the crate.

Prepare your crate by placing it in an area of your home where you or your family spend a lot of time. Place a towel or soft blanket inside. Open the crate and allow your dog to explore it. While some are naturally curious and will enter and sleep inside right away, some may be more hesitant.

If your dog is one of the hesitant ones, talk to him or her in a happy tone and bring them over to the crate. Make sure that the door of the crate is open. Encourage your pet to enter the crate by creating a food trail that ends inside the crate. If your Australian Shepherd refuses to go all the way in during the first try, do not force him or her to enter. Be patient and try again. Consistently create a food trail or even throw in treats inside the crate until your pet walks inside willingly. Also, take note that some dogs are not interested in treats, so you may be better off throwing in their favorite toy inside the crate.

2. Feed your dog inside or near the crate.

After introducing your Australian Shepherd into his or her crate, start feeding them their meals near the crate. This will help them associate crate training with something pleasant and positive. If your dog is willing to enter the crate, place his food all the way inside.

Once your pet is comfortable eating inside the crate, close the door while he or she is busy with his or her food. During the first times you do this, open the crate door as soon as they finish eating. With each following feed, leave the door closed for a few minutes longer until your Australian Shepherd is inside the crate 10 minutes or more after he or she finishes.

If your Australian Shepherd begins to whine because he or she wants to get out, let your pet out. You may have kept him or her inside too long, so cut the time the next time you do your training. If your dog tends to keep on whining or crying no matter how short he or she is inside the crate, don't let your pet out until he or she stops. Letting him or her out right away if your pet tends to whine will make him or her realize that whining will always get him or her what he or she wants.

3. Practice for longer periods.

Once you know that your Australian Shepherd is comfortable eating inside his or her crate and shows no anxiousness or fear, you can contain him in the crate for short periods of time.

Call him over to the crate and give your pet a treat. You can use the command "kennel" and then encourage them to enter the crate by pointing inside. Once your pet is inside the crate, praise him or her, give the treat and then close the door. Sit near the crate for around 5 or 10 minutes and then leave the room for a few minutes. Once you return, sit near the crate again for a short time and then let your Australian Shepherd out.

Repeat this training several times a day, gradually increasing the time he or she is inside the crate and the time you are out of sight.

4. Crate when you leave...

Once your dog can spend around half an hour inside the crate without feeling fearful or nervous, you can start leaving them inside the crate for short periods when you leave the house. You can opt to leave some treats inside the crate, and even add some of his favorite toys inside as well.

Do not make your departures long and emotional. Leave without making a big fuss. Praise your dog, give a treat and then leave. When you get home, do not be overexcited. Keep it low-key to avoid making them anxious for your return the next time you leave again.

5. ...And crate at night.

On the other hand, you are using the crate as your dog's bedroom, place it inside your own room or in a nearby hall. This is especially relevant if you have a puppy or older dog. Puppies tend to whine at night when they want to be let out to relieve themselves, while older dogs might associate crate training with isolation if you are not nearby.

Once your Australian Shepherd is comfortable sleeping through the night inside his or her crate, slowly move it to your preferred location. Remember though that sleeping near each other is a way you can further strengthen your bond with your Australian Shepherd.

Teaching Your Dog to Herd

Australian Shepherds were bred to herd. With the right training, patience and encouragement, you can actually bring out your pet's herding instincts. Through some basic training exercises and basic obedience training, you can assess whether your dog has future in herding. If he or she displays potential for herding, you can consider detailed tutorials on herding or even seek the help of a professional trainer.

Here are some steps you can take if you want your Australian Shepherd to learn how to herd:

1. Make sure you train your dog basic training tricks because dogs who are unable to be obedient off-leash and listen to you despite outside distractions, herding will be a nearly impossible skill to teach.
2. Assess your dog's behavior. Australian Shepherds who have solid herding instincts will be able to showcase this skill early on even without training. The way to assess your dog is to observe whether he or she moves around you and other animals in a circular motion.

3. Remember that the earlier you teach your dog to herd, the better he or she will be at it. While you can certainly teach your dog how to herd, a professional trainer will more likely be more effective at it especially if you have never trained another dog to herd in the past.

4. Play catch with your dog or start teaching your Australian Shepherd how to retrieve balls and other toys for you. As soon as possible, teach your dog to only retrieve his or her toy when you command it.

5. Teach your Australian Shepherd directional movement, that is, how to go left or right. Use a leash and walk your pet through the said motions while saying "left" or "right" so he or she associates the words with the movement.

6. After your dog learns left and right, teach him or her how to run clockwise when you say "bye" and counterclockwise when you say "way". Also get him or her used to stopping and lying down when you say "wait" or a similar command.

7. Get your Australian Shepherd familiar with livestock. Get your pet used to obeying your commands while he or she is around other animals. If you don't own livestock, get in touch with local dog herding associations to find out where you can expose your Australian Shepherd to livestock.

8. Teach your dog how to herd a real animal. Either purchase or get access to a duck or lamb for your Australian Shepherd to practice herding on. Place the animals in a small kennel while practicing basic commands on your dog. Get them familiar and comfortable with each other.

9. Observe your dog's body language. If a dog has a natural instinct for herding, his or her tail will go down when around

the flock. This is an indication that your dog is analyzing the situation. He or she should naturally run in circles around the other animals and he or she will respond to your commands. Respect your dog's natural limits. Remember not all Australian Shepherds will have the knack for herding even if they were bred to herd.

10. Progress to more complex commands once your dog shows obedience, knows basic commands, and is more familiar with livestock. Get your dog to run around the herd, but also help him or her develop the ability to move from place to place.

Here is a practical application of basic commands when it comes to herding:

a. Outrun: An extremely vital skill, your Australian Shepherd should be able to run past the herd and stop them from moving away. This shows that he or she can get the livestock under control.

b. The lift: Introducing himself or herself to the flock, this move will push the flock to respect your Australian Shepherd and follow his or her directions.

c. The fetch: This move sees your Australian Shepherd herding the flock back to you.

11. Enroll yourself and your dog in classes because the basic commands will only get you so far when it comes to herding. This is especially relevant if you want your pet to learn more advanced commands or you want your Australian Shepherd to be involved in dog shows.

How to Join a Dog Show

One of the most popular dog activities around is dog showing. Not only will you be able to showcase your dog's physicality and skills, but you will also be able to interact with other dog enthusiasts. All purebred, pedigree dogs can join dog shows.

Taking place in different rings at a dog show, pedigrees are judges against their Breed Standards. Considered as the blueprint for the ideal characteristics (including temperament and health) for each breed, dogs who are close to the Breed Standards receive top awards.

Truth be told, it is rather easy to get started in dog showing. Here are some of the things you need to do if you want to be part of this sport:

1. Register your dog with the Kennel Club on the Breed Register. Make sure that your Australian Shepherd is 6 months or older.
2. Enter a show in a class that is appropriate for your pet.
3. Your dog's health is extremely important if you want to join a dog show. Make sure your dog is healthy, free of illness and happy before joining.
4. Prepare to join a dog show by first visiting a show or multiple shows to see what dog showing is all about. Once you see a show, you will have a better regarding the characteristics judges look for in each dog or even more specifically, what they look for in Australian Shepherds.
5. Take note of the Breed Standards for Australian Shepherds and see how your pet lives up to the said standards.
6. Attend a class specifically intended for show training to learn more about how to present your dog at a show.
7. Join a show and enjoy!

CHAPTER 11

Australian Shepherd Lifespan and Health

The Australian Shepherd is naturally athletic and thrives in physical activity and hard work. Because of this dog's build and penchant for exercise and sport, he tends to be a healthier and sturdier breed than others. However, while Australian Shepherds do tend to be a fit lot, they can still be afflicted with health conditions just like any other creature.

Australian Shepherds are a fit lot, but they can still be afflicted with certain health conditions.

This chapter seeks to give you answers regarding health issues your dog may have, and some health exams you can give your dog to keep in in as healthy a state as possible. A special section is also dedicated to the so-called lethal white or double merle Australian Shepherd who suffers from blindness and deafness.

Also, this chapter gives you some tips on how to deal with the loss of a beloved pet, the sorrow felt by many pet owners once their beloved Australian Shepherd passes, and the remembrance and celebration of the love and happiness given to you by your beloved Australian Shepherd.

Australian Shepherd Health Issues and Tests

Like other dog breeds (and human beings), Australian Shepherds have the potential to develop genetic health problems. Because of this potential for inherited health issues, never do business with a breeder who cannot offer a health guarantee on his or her puppies. Or one who tells you that the breed is 100 percent healthy and has no potential to develop health issues in the future, and who has puppies that are isolated from other dogs due to health problems. Reputable breeders will give you paperwork regarding their dogs' health and they will be open and honest with you about the health problems associated with Australian Shepherds.

Although Australian Shepherds are generally healthy dogs, they can still develop particular conditions such as hip dysplasia, certain eye diseases, hyperthyroidism, epilepsy, cancer and even sensitivity to some drugs.

Established in 2002, the Australian Shepherd Health & Genetics Institute (ASHGI), is dedicated to working with canine health organizations and foundations, researchers and breed clubs to raise money for genetic health research for the dog breed. According to the organization, "Without research, specific to Aussies, modes of inheritance will not be determined for this breed nor will DNA screening tests be developed."

Here are brief descriptions of these health conditions as well as the health exams and screening tests that your Australian Shepherd may require:

1. Hip Dysplasia

A genetic malformation of the hip socket, hip dysplasia is further aggravated if a dog is overweight or obese. Typically, dogs with hip dysplasia look normal; however, over time, the cartilage on the surface of the thigh bone wears away because its head does not fit perfectly into the hip socket. This then leads to inflammation, which then results in arthritis.

This condition can range from mild to severe. While some dogs tolerate mild hip dysplasia, severe cases typically need to be corrected surgically. Most of the time, surgery means a total hip replacement which costs thousands of dollars. If an owner refuses to treat this condition, this refusal is tantamount to cruelty as the dog will suffer severe pain and may even be unable to move. Usually diagnosed by manual manipulation of the hips and X-rays, this health condition can be so painful that diagnosis may even require anesthesia.

*Typically, dogs with hip dysplasia look normal but
the condition worsens over time and can lead to arthritis.*

You will not be able to tell if your Australian Shepherd has hip
dysplasia by simply watching or observing your pet move or walk.
If you purchase a dog from a thorough and reputable breeder,
he or she will be able to tell you and give you proof if your
prospective pet has hips rated "good" or better by the Orthopedic
Foundation for Animals (OFA) or the University of Pennsylvania
(PennHIP).

2. Eye Diseases

Common afflictions that affect Australian Shepherds are
genetic eye problems. Eye conditions that affect this dog breed
include Iris Coloboma, Progressive Retinal Atrophy (PRA),
cataracts, Persistent Pupillary Membrane (PPM), and Collie
Eye Anomaly (CEA).

Iris Coloboma

A condition characterized by the failure of the iris to develop, it is present at birth. Notches on the iris can be small, but there are cases that the notches are so large that dogs appear that they have no irises at all. While this condition does not affect the vision of Australian Shepherds in most cases, large coloboma can force a dog to squint when presented with bright light because the iris is not capable of properly contracting which then reduces the amount of light that is able to enter the eyes. This difficulty results in minor discomfort and even a reduction in a dog's range of vision.

An ophthalmologic exam can usually help detect this condition, but owners and vets can sometimes visually see right away if there is something wrong with the Australian Shepherd's irises. The mode of inheritance for this condition is currently unknown. Affected animals are not supposed to be bred.

While Iris Coloboma is characterized by missing parts of the iris, Iris Hypoplasia is a condition that leads to the thinning of the iris tissue. It is currently unknown if Iris Hypoplasia is simply a milder version of Iris Coloboma. Dogs with this condition can be bred but only with mates that do not have the condition or a family history of Iris Hypoplasia.

Progressive Retinal Atrophy (PRA)

Progressive Retinal Atrophy (PRA) is the gradual degeneration of the retinal tissue. Caused be a recessive gene mutation, the PRA form found in Australian Shepherds is referred to as Progressive Rod Cone Degeneration (PRCD). Typically occurring during the prime of the dog's life, the first thing the owner notices about his or her pet is that the dog suddenly has night-blindness. In a matter of months or years, the disease progresses, leaving the dog blind.

Because Progressive Rod Cone Degeneration is progressive, multiple examinations are needed to confirm it. An Australian Shepherd diagnosed with Progressive Retinal Atrophy should be given the PRCD DNA test to confirm the diagnosis as the condition tends to be misdiagnosed.

Good breeders know that dogs with this affliction should not be bred, and carriers of the gene can be bred but only with mates who are clear of the disease. The offspring of carriers need to be tested as well.

Cataracts

Considered as the most common eye disease in Australian Shepherds, this condition can be caused by heredity, injury, nutritional imbalance or other diseases. While the disease can result from other issues other than genetics, heredity is still the usual cause.

Hereditary cataracts are referred to as bilateral because they occur in both eyes, although they sometimes appear at different times. If cataracts are found in one eye, the other eye should be checked again in 6 months to a year to see if cataracts develop. These types of cataracts begin with the eye looking opaque which could look like a clouding of the eye lens. Australian Shepherds with this condition are unable to visually decipher anything except extreme light or extreme dark. While this condition leads to loss of vision, it is not painful. This condition does not usually affect puppies, but more mature dogs.

The majority of cataracts in Australian Shepherds have posterior polar cortical cataracts, meaning the condition occurs on the back side in the center of the outer layer of the cortex. The mode of inheritance for Australian Shepherds is dominant with incomplete penetrance which means that not all dogs with this genetic mutation will develop cataracts.

In early 2008, a DNA test for hereditary cataracts was created to reduce the frequency of cataracts in Australian Shepherds. It was discovered that a mutation in a gene called HSF4 is associated with 70 percent of inherited cataracts in this dog breed. The HSF4 gene mutation is dominant, so dogs who have even one copy of it is at risk of developing cataracts at some point in their lives. The mutation is risky – meaning, even if two dogs who have the gene mutation but do not have cataracts breed, their offspring could still potentially develop the condition. In fact, the mutation is so common in the breed that 1 in 4 Australian Shepherds have it.

While the HSF4 gene mutation poses a risk for cataracts, there are other hereditary cataracts not caused by it. All Australian Shepherds that are to be bred should then be examined annually by a veterinary ophthalmologist.

Persistent Pupillary Membrane (PPM)

Before a puppy is born, his or her pupil is covered with a pupillary membrane. The said fetal structure should go away shortly after the dog is born; however, in some cases some part or all the membrane will remain. This is referred to as Persistent Pupillary Membrane (PPM).

Most cases of Persistent Pupillary Membrane do not cause substantial visual impairment; however, in some dogs the condition may cause some level of blindness especially if the membrane is attached to the cornea or lens. The condition is hereditary if it has not gone away by the time an Australian Shepherd turns 1.

In puppies, the condition is not a major concern as they may just be going through some developmental delays which lead to portions of the membrane staying longer than usual. Puppies with Persistent Pupillary Membrane should be examined again after 6 months to a year. If the condition resolves itself by year one, there is nothing to be concerned about. Should the condition remain after a year, it can cause some level of blindness in the Australian Shepherd.

Australian Shepherds with Persistent Pupillary Membrane that attaches to the lens or cornea should not be bred. Should breeders opt to breed dogs with other types of Persistent Pupillary Membrane, it is advised that the dogs not be bred with their own pedigrees or with mates who have a history of the condition.

Collie Eye Anomaly (CEA)

A congenital inherited eye condition, Collie Eye Anomaly (CEA) can at times lead to blindness. Only 25 percent of puppies from two carriers will be affected by the said condition.

Dogs with this disease also have Bilateral Choroidal Hypoplasia (CH) or Chorioretinal Dysplasia. Bilateral Choroidal Hypoplasia or Chorioretinal Dysplasia is the thinning of the vascular tissue in the back of the eye. These conditions do not really affect vision that much, and can be apparent in puppies over 6-8 weeks of age.

Other dogs with Collie Eye Anomaly will also have Optic Nerve Coloboma, which results in the failure of nerve tissues to fully develop. On the other hand, a few will have retinal detachment.

Both Optic Nerve Coloboma and retinal detachment are serious conditions which can lead to blindness. Both can only be diagnosed through an eye exam.

Present at birth, Collie Eye Anomaly does not progress. The condition does not worsen as puppies get older, and it does not cause any pain. As a matter of fact, Australian Shepherd puppies with this condition look normal as only a few with Collie Eye Anomaly will experience impaired vision. Defects are found inside the eye and can old by detected with special instruments by a veterinarian ophthalmologist or through a DNA test.

Easily missed, breeders should routinely do eye examination on their puppies to look for Collie Eye Anomaly.

This long list of eye issues then necessitates breeders to take extreme care when it comes to making sure that their Australian Shepherds have no genetic predispositions or conditions when it comes to their vision and eye structures. When opting to purchase from a breeder, make sure that your prospective pet has been certified to have normal eyes by a board-certified veterinary ophthalmologist. The results of the exam done on your dog must be recorded with the Canine Eye Registry Foundation (CERF).

Aside from screening the parents for eye disease, all the puppies in the litter should have their eyes examined by a veterinary ophthalmologist after six weeks of age and before you bring them home. As an owner, you should also have your Australian Shepherd's eyes checked every year by a veterinary ophthalmologist to make sure your pet does not develop any eye conditions.

3. Hyperthyroidism

Considered as the most common autoimmune disease in Australian Shepherds, thyroid disease is fortunately treatable and medication is usually expensive. However, caring breeders still take steps to avoid producing dogs that are afflicted with this condition.

The condition is so common that vets tend to either over-diagnose or under-diagnose their canine patients. Some vets may diagnose the disease by default if a dog shows symptoms such as a tendency to seek heat, weight gain and skin issues. But while hyperthyroidism could be a disease in itself, it could sometimes just be a symptom of an underlying issue. A dog can be diagnosed with a thyroid problem when he or she is actually ill from another disease or if a female dog is simply going through her estrus cycle. Only thorough examination and testing done by a vet can determine whether a dog has a thyroid disease or not.

Because the disease is so common, all dogs that are intended to be bred should be screened when they turn 1 or 2 years old, and then every year after until they reach 4 years old. After 4, a thyroid testing panel similar to the mandatory one by the Orthopedic Foundation for Animals should be done at ages 2, 3, 4 and 6. Should the results indicate the presence of T3, T4, or thyroglobulin autoantibodies above reference range (T4 AA >20, T3 AA >10, TGAA >35), then the dog is affected. If until the age of 6, the Australian Shepherd is clear in all tests, then he or she is not affected by the condition.

It should be noted that female dogs who suffer from thyroid disease could potentially experience problems with their reproductive system.

Both male and female dogs with this condition should be withheld from breeding. Also, because the condition is typically prevalent within a family, those who have relatives which have hyperthyroidism should only breed with mates with normal thyroid screening tests and who have no family history of the condition.

4. Epilepsy

While this condition occurs in Australian Shepherds, there is currently no screening test for seizure disorders in the breed. It is good to note that epilepsy is rare in Australian puppies that are younger than 1 year old. The disease is also rare in adult dogs older than 7 years old.

Seizures should never be ignored. Take your dog to the vet right away.

Remember that seizures should never be ignored. A dog that suffers a major episode should be taken to the vet right away so he or she can be tested and examined. Caused by a variety of reasons such as disease, exposure to toxins, injury and heredity, the vet rules out possible causes of the seizure when treating the dog. Depending on the health history of the dog, as well as his or her family history, a variety of tests will be done on him or her. When all other likely causes of the seizure are rules on, the veterinary will more likely diagnose the dog as having epilepsy.

Remember that primary epilepsy has no cure, and your dog's seizure will worsen if he or she is not given medication. While medication can help alleviate and lessen the intensity of a dog's seizures, the dog may still experience seizures periodically throughout his or her life.

Around 4 percent of Australian Shepherds have epilepsy, and is a condition that is inherited. At this time, there is no DNA test for epilepsy in Australian Shepherds.

5. Cancer

A common ailment in dogs, cancer is also the most common natural cause of death in canines, particularly in elderly dogs. However, cancer can also affect younger dogs especially in some breeds that are more genetically predisposed to the condition.

While many may think that cancer is one disease, it is actually classified as any disease that has to do with the uncontrolled proliferation of abnormal cells. When this occurs, the said cells could potentially create a tumor which could then metastasize, sending these abnormal cells throughout the body to wreak havoc.

All cancers find their root in genetic mutations, although these mutations are not always inherited. As a matter of fact, most are not inherited, but rather, these abnormal cells accumulate in the body over time due to exposure to radioactive substances, particular chemicals or even too much sunlight. Exposure to these factors could scramble your Australian Shepherd's DNA, and over time, his or her scrambled DNA is repeatedly copied in the body.

While breeders can do their best to make sure that their dogs are as healthy as possible, they can only do so much when it comes to preventing their animals from exposure to environmental carcinogens. Also, they have no control when it comes to preventing DNA copying errors. All breeders can do is to be knowledgeable about their dogs inherited predispositions and what cancers Australian Shepherds are more prone to.

One devastating form of canine cancer that is becoming more and more prevalent in Australian Shepherds is hemangiosarcoma. Hemangiosarcoma is a malignant tumor of blood vessel cells. Because tumors begin in blood vessels, they are typically filled with blood; and when tumors rupture, they cause internal or external bleeding. This form of cancer is aggressive, has no cure or hope for recovery, and has no known cause although many vets believe that heredity plays a huge role in it.

6. Sensitivity to Drugs

Some Australian Shepherds have fatal reactions to some veterinary drugs due to a genetic mutation. One of the drugs that Australian Shepherds can be sensitive to is Ivermectin, a drug used to prevent heartworm.

To find out if your dog is sensitive to particular drugs, screening him or her as well as his or her parents is necessary. Screening is a simple and easy cheek swab, the sample of which is then sent to go through an extremely accurate DNA test. The said DNA test will identify the genotype or form of the Multi-Drug Resistance (MDR1) gene the dog has. Dogs who have the said mutation will have a transport defect in their bodies, meaning the drug they ingest goes directly to their brains and fail to be transported to the rest of their bodies. This failure to transport then builds up the level of toxicity in the brain, resulting in neurological problems such as seizures and something death.

If dogs are sensitive to drugs, owners are encouraged to place a medic alert type collar on their pets for safety's sake.

The Lethal White/Double Merle

The merle allele influences the pigmentation of dogs, giving them light or white areas.

A double merle Australian Shepherd is sometimes referred to as lethal white; however, the lethal white term is inaccurate. The term lethal white implies that double merle Australian Shepherds do not live long, which is simply not true. Double merles do have the same lifespans as standard Australian Shepherds.

A healthy merle Australian Shepherd received the merle allele from only one of his or her parents. While in the case of a double merle, the merle allele is received from both parents, giving the Australian Shepherd a double dose.

The merle allele influences the pigmentation of dogs, giving them light or white areas. In single inheritances, Australian Shepherds only display patches of white or light; while double inheritances see dogs having the predominantly white color.

While the predominant white color can be striking, double merles have to contend with particular health problems that the typical Australian Shepherd may not have. These health issues can vary from mild to severe, with some puppies being born either deaf or blind or in worst cases, both.

Here are the descriptions of the audio and visual impairments double merles could suffer from:

1. Audio Impairment or Deafness

This condition typically develops after an Australian Shepherd puppy is born. This is the time in a dog's life that his or her ear canal is still closed.

The white color of double merles is produced due to the lack of melanocytes or pigment-producing cells. Melanocytes are responsible for providing high levels of potassium in the endolymph or fluid that surrounds the hair cells of the cochlea. When there is a lack or absence of melanocytes, blood supply to the cochlea is compromised, the stria vacularis is affected and the end result is that the nerve cells of the cochlea die, leading to permanent deafness. There is no treatment or surgery that can reduce the said damage.

Hearing loss is directly related to how much pigmentation cells a dog has. If some pigmentation cells are present, the dog can still have some level of hearing. Without the said cells, the dog will be totally deaf. This can occur in one or both ears.

Deafness is not only dangerous for the dog since he or she will be unable to hear nearby cars or animals, but it is also dangerous for anyone who encounters the dog because a person can unknowingly startle the animal. This is particularly concerning when children interact with deaf dogs as children may be a bit less cautious when playing with the animals.

2. Visual Impairment or Blindness

Double merle Australian Shepherds can have vision problems, including total blindness.

These dogs can suffer from vision conditions such as cataracts, retinal detachment, Iris Coloboma, Persistent Pupillary Membrane, a displacement of the lens, Equatorial Staphyloma, night blindness and others.

The same pigment lacking in the ears can also be lacking in the eyes, thus affecting their development. This development begins when the dog is still an embryo, and the damage to the eyes will depend on when the development is compromised.

When it comes to double merles, sometimes the growth of one eye is impeded, while other cases may have dogs having one eye that is smaller than the other (microopthalmia) or two eyes missing (anopthalmia).

Aside from these conditions, double merles also suffer from other eye conditions such as hypoplasia, or a starburst or sunburst pupil wherein the pupil is not properly formed and looks as if it has rays surrounding the iris. Dogs who suffer from these conditions have a difficult time being exposed to bright lights.

Although many believe that eye problems only occur in dogs with blue eyes, this is simply not true. What is true that due to the contrast created with eye issues and blue eyes, eye conditions are just a lot easier to spot in blue-eyed dogs.

Australian Shepherd Lifespan and Dealing with Grief

Like other medium to large dog breeds, the Australian Shepherd typically has a lifespan of around 13 to 15 years. While having a dog certainly adds more energy and purpose to a lot of people's lives, death is certainly part of the equation. Pets are more likely to pass before their owners, and it certainly can be a difficult grieving process if your Australian Shepherd has truly become a member of the family.

Know that sorrow and grief are normal responses to death. Your furry friend has been part of your life and your family, and you consider him or her to be a loved one. Because of this, losing a pet can certainly be painful and devastating and can only be dealt with over time.

Here are some ways you can cope with the loss and sadness:

1. **Do not allow anyone to tell you that you shouldn't feel the loss – even yourself.**

   Other people don't really see what the big deal is when it comes to the loss of a pet. Some would say that dogs are just animals and not human beings; therefore, you shouldn't really be grieving over the loss. Do not allow anyone to downplay your grief. Your pet was part of your family. Do not feel embarrassed feeling sad. It's okay to feel angry and devastated. It's okay to cry.

2. **Reach out to other people who will understand.**

   Other people have gone through what you are going through. Reach out to other pet owners online, attend pet support groups, and talk with friends or family members who will be sympathetic to your loss. Ask for support from people who will understand the pain and sorrow you are going through.

3. **Rituals can help you deal with the loss.**

   While some may laugh at the idea of holding a funeral for a deceased pet, rituals such as this can help with your healing. Funerals and memorials allow you to openly express how you feel about your beloved Australian Shepherd. Although it may prove to be difficult, ignore the people who think a funeral or memorial are ridiculous. Do whatever you feel is right for you.

4. **Preserve memories.**

   Whether it be compiling photos of your Australian Shepherd, planting a tree in memory of your pet, or keeping your pet's favorite toys inside a memory box, preserve memories of your dog and celebrate his or her life. He or she was a part of your life, home and family, and preserving memories can help you create a legacy which you can go back to time and time again and can help you move forward.

5. Take care of yourself.

Losing a pet can cause stress and emotional devastation. Look after your physical and emotional needs even if it is hard. Eat healthy, sleep, exercise and look for ways in which you can boost your mood.

6. If you have other pets, do not forget about taking care of them as well.

In as much as the loss of a pet can cause you stress, your other pets can also feel sad and stressed from the loss and from your sadness. Maintain your daily routine and do not forget to take care of and nurture your other pets. Interact with them even more during this difficult time. Not only will this help elevate your outlook and mood, it will benefit your surviving pets as well.

7. Ask for professional help if you need it.

As mentioned, the loss of a pet can be painful. It is still the loss of a loved one. Some people can deal with the loss on their own, but others are not able to get out of the gloom. If you feel extremely depressed and you feel that you cannot deal with the loss on your own, seek professional help. There is no shame in it. You need to be able to talk to someone about your feelings so you can move forward.

CHAPTER 12

Conclusion

The Australian Shepherd is an athletic, active and energetic dog breed that loves to work, socialize and bond with his or her family. Once you've decided to bring home your new pet home, you will find out how truly challenging yet rewarding it is to raise your new family member, and how wonderful it is to welcome him or her into your family. While your dog may want to assert his or her dominance over you, once you show him or her who's boss, his or her love and devotion will make you wonder why you haven't considered getting an Australian Shepherd a long time ago.

Owning the beautifully striking Australian Shepherd, l ike any other dog breed, is a long-term commitment.

While the Australian Shepherd is naturally athletic and sturdy, he or she is prone to some serious health issues specific to its breed. Make sure to give him or her the nutrition and exercise he or she needs, and screen him or her regularly for conditions common in his or her breed.

Owning the beautifully striking Australian Shepherd, like any other dog breed, is a long-term commitment. It is a responsibility that necessitates your time and energy to make sure that your dog is nurtured through proper nutrition and exercise, trained and loved.

Good luck and enjoy the years to come with your Australian Shepherd!

If you enjoyed this book would you mind leaving a very quick review on http://www.amazon.com ?

It means so much Thank you! Mark Manfield ☺

Your Trusted Resource List

This trusted resource list will help you further maximize your experience with the Australian Shepherd breed. Enjoy!

Breeders USA (in alphabetical order):

- **Animali**
  http://www.aussieforme.com
  USA Breeder, Based in California, also provides stud service

- **Aussbern**
  http://aussbernsaussies.com
  USA Breeder, Based in Illinois, AKC Breeder Of Merit

- **Buff Cap**
  http://www.buffcap.com
  USA Breeder, Based in Connecticut, ASCA Hall of Fame

- **Calais**
  http://www.calaisaussies.com
  USA Breeder, Based in Colorado, AKC Breeder Of Merit
  and Hall of Fame Kennel

- **Casa Blanca**
  http://www.CasaBlancaAussies.com
  USA Breeder, Based in California, AKC Hall of Fame Kennel

- **Chances R Aussies**
  http://www.chancesraussies.com
  USA Breeder, Based in California, AKC Breeder Of Merit

- **Collinswood K-9 Services**
  http://www.collinswoodk9.com
  USA Breeder, Based in Massachusetts, also offers grooming services and has indoor training facility, boarding and daycare

- **Copper Hill Aussies**
  http://www.copperhillaussies.com
  USA Breeder, Based in Florida, AKC Breeder Of Merit, Hall of Fame Kennel, Puppies, Conformation, Performance

- **Eaglecrest**
  http://www.eaglecrestaussies.com
  USA Breeder, Based in California, AKC Breeder Of Merit Participant

- **Equinox**
  http://www.equinoxaussies.com
  USA Breeder, Based in Virginia, Hall of Fame Kennel

- **Fairview**
  http://www.fairviewaustralianshepherds.com
  USA Breeder, Based in Florida, AKC Breeder Of Merit

- **Flat Rock**
  http://www.flat-rock-dogs.com
  USA Breeder, Based in Georgia, AKC Breeder Of Merit

- **Fiddlers Green**
  http://www.fiddlersgreenaussies.net
  USA Breeder, Based in Colorado, AKC Breeder Of Merit

- **Graffiti**
  http://www.graffitiaussies.com
  USA Breeder, Based in Missouri, AKC Breeder Of Merit

- **Heartfire**
  http://www.heartfirefarms.com
  USA Breeder, Based in California, Breeder of Australian Shepherds since 1981

- **Hearthside**
  http://www.hearthsideaussies.com
  USA Breeder, Based in New York, AKC Breeder Of Merit

- **IndigoMoon**
  http://www.indigomoonaussies.com
  USA Breeder, Based in Arkansas, occasionally sells adult Australian Shepherds

- **Jamara**
  http://www.jamara-australianshepherds.com
  USA Breeder, Based in California, offers stud service and occasionally sells adult Australian Shepherds

- **Lakehills**
  http://www.lakehillaussies.com
  USA Breeder, Based in California, Owned by Lisa Renville, an ASCA Senior Breeder Judge

- **Limelite**
  http://www.limeliteaussies.com
  USA Breeder, Based in California, AKC Breeder Of Merit

- **McMatt**
  http://www.mcmattaussies.com
  USA Breeder, Based in Illinois, AKC Breeder Of Merit

- **MontRose**
  http://www.montroseaussies.com
  USA Breeder, Based in New York, AKC Breeder Of Merit and involved in the breed for over 25 years and produced dogs titled in various venues with a concentration on conformation

- **Narita Farms**
  http://www.naritafarmsaussies.com
  USA Breeder, Based in Arizona, also sells Border Collies, Sheep, Goats, Ducks and Other Dog-related Merchandise

- **Oakhurst**
  http://www.oakhurstaussies.com
  USA Breeder, Based in Maryland, AKC Breeder Of Merit and offers grooming services

- **Old West**
  http://www.oldwestaussies.com
  USA Breeder, Based in California, breeders of multiple champion & titled Australian Shepherds in both ASCA and AKC

- **Poise Aussies**
  http://www.poiseaussies.com
  USA Breeder, Based in Texas, guarantees CERF, PRA, CEA, HSF4, MDR1 tested

- **Red Forrest**
  http://www.redforrestaussies.com
  USA Breeder, Based in California, owned by Laura Diebold, Senior Breeder Judge

- **Richwood**
  http://www.richwoodfarms.com
  USA Breeder, Based in Michigan, Breeder since 1972, AKC Breeder Of Merit and offers all colors

- **Ryan Creek**
  http://www.ryancreekaussies.com
  USA Breeder, Based in Alabama, AKC Breeder Of Merit
- **SummeReane**
  http://www.SummeReaneKennels.com
  USA Breeder, Based in Alabama, AKC Breeder Of Merit

BREEDERS CANADA:

- **CedarPaws**
  http://http://www.cedarpaws.ca
  Canada Breeder, based in Toronto, Ontario.

BREEDERS UK:

- **Amberslade**
  http://www.amberslade.co.uk
  UK Breeders, New Forest, Hampshire

BREED SPECIFIC FURTHER RESOURCES:

"Active Aussies."
  http://www.australianshepherdsfurever.org/active-aussies
  Activities Australian Shepherds thrive in.

"Aussie Info."
  http://aussieinfo.org/
  An extensive collection of articles and photos on working Aussies.

"Aussie Rescue & Placement Helpline (ARPH)."
  http://www.aussierescue.org/
  Dedicated volunteers seeking to rescue purebred Australian Shepherds and find them forever homes.

"Australian Shepherd Club of America (ASCA)."
  http://www.asca.org/
  The independent Aussie registry, unaffiliated with AKC.

"Australian Shepherd Genetics Institute (ASHGI)."
http://www.ashgi.org/
The center for current, scientific information about Aussie genetic health issues.

"Australian Shepherd Lovers."
http://www.australian-shepherd-lovers.com/

"Australian Shepherd Pedigree Search."
http://pedigrees.theaustralianshepherd.net/
Pedigree research.

"Good Boy: Best Dog Food for Australian Shepherds."
https://herepup.com/best-dog-food-for-australian-shepherds/

"Good Mates: The Best Toys for Australian Shepherds."
https://herepup.com/best-toys-for-australian-shepherds/

"Raising an Australian Shepherd: Temperament and Development."
http://www.k9station.com/articles/raisinganaussie.htm

"Training Australian Shepherds."
http://www.yourpurebredpuppy.com/training/australian shepherds.html

"United States Australian Shepherd Association (USASA)."
http://www.australianshepherds.org/
Dedicated to promoting, preserving, and protecting the Australian Shepherd breed.

"Working Aussie Source."
http://www.workingaussiesource.com/
The group's goal is to be the source of information and inspiration for those who want to utilize the breed for livestock management.